Dream Healing Practitioner Guidebook

A Healer's Guide to Uncovering
the Secret Messages of Your Dreams

Wendie Webber

Dream Healing Practitioner Guidebook: *A Healer's Guide to Uncovering the Secret Messages of Your Dreams*

Wendie Webber

Copyright © 2023 Wendie Webber
All Rights Reserved.

All rights reserved. No part of this publication may be reproduced, distributed, or transmitted in any form or by any means, including photocopying, recording, or other electronic or mechanical methods without the prior written permission from the author, except in the case of brief quotations embodied in critical reviews and certain non-commercial uses permitted by copyright law.

The information given in this book should not be treated as a substitute for professional medical advice; always consult a medical practitioner. Any use of information in this book is at the reader's discretion and risk. Neither the author nor the publisher can be held responsible for any loss, claim, or damage arising out of the use, or misuse, of the suggestions made, the failure to take medical advice, or for any material on third-party websites.

ISBN Print Book: 978-1-7774121-8-0

What Others Say...

"Flabbergasted..."

I was flabbergasted by the tools of *Dream Healing*. Wendie is an amazing teacher, so knowledgeable, and able to bring so much clarity to complex themes while making it fun to learn and practice. She guided me through not just how to interpret my dreams but also how to sleep and awaken better, remember, and journal my dreams. *Dream Healing* is a deep journey into your subconscious that allows you to understand what your many inner parts want to communicate with you to change your life.

Marta Santos Lima
Hipnoterapeuta Alquimica (Transpessoal)
Porto, Portugal

"The Magic of It All Is Just Plain Fun"

Wendie Webber is, hands down, the expert in the field of dream healing. I'd been working with dreams for decades before I discovered her work. And to say I learned things I'd never heard of before is an understatement. What she taught me opened up a dialogue with my subconscious mind that has helped me immensely in my waking life. My intuition is stronger, my work is more effective, and the magic of it all is just plain fun.

Sharon Jackman, Hypnosis Specialist for Women

"Knowledge of Dream Interpretation Is Spot On..."

Wow, does this gal know about dreams! Wendie explains in imagery and details how to interpret a dream. Her knowledge of dream interpretation is spot on. She opens the doors of our subconscious imagination to explore the feelings expressed in our dreams. I enthusiastically recommend Wendie Webber's Dream Healing course.

Gena Kidd
Integrative Wellness
Shelbyville, KY

"Makes Things So Simple and Easy . . ."

I have thoroughly loved working with Wendie Webber's dream healing tools. Wendie makes things so simple and easy that learning new skills, such as dream healing, becomes easy to apply and implement from the start. I have absolutely loved uncovering my dream meanings and then putting what I've learned into action because understanding a dream is not enough. It also needs some change/action for resolution to happen. It's been such an interesting and fun experience. Thank you so much, Wendie!

Nicole Dodd, Hypnotist
Mindset for Change
Norfolk, UK

"Life-Changing, Eye-Opening, Mind-Blowing . . ."

Almost everyone knows that dreams are the language of the subconscious mind . . . and many would interpret their dreams in many ways . . . but few would know how to ride their dreams in a lucid way. Then, there are the elite few who know how to use the power of the subconscious language of dreams for therapy. If you are a therapist, go on a life-changing, eye-opening, mind-blowing experience with Wendie Webber and learn how to be a Dream Healing Practitioner. A training course like no other -- for the elite few.

Daniel Ghanime
The Control Alternative
Lebanon

Contents

Why Read This Book 1
Are you a hypnosis practitioner? 3
Hypnotherapy Is Dream Healing 4
What You Will Learn 5

Why Dreams? 7
When we sleep, we dream. 7
How much sleep? 11
Sleep cycles 12
Why do we dream? 14
What is a dream? 15
This Dream 15
Day Dream 16
Night Dream 16
What equipment do you need? 16
Summary 17

A Brief History 19
Babylonians 19
Egyptians 20
Greeks 23
Romans 23
Hebrews 24
Hawaiian 26

Australian 27

Native American 27

Summary 28

Two Minds 29

Summary 32

A Dream Is a Story 33

Types of Dreams 34

    Venting Dreams 34

    Problem-Solving Dreams 35

    Nightmares 36

    Factual Dreams 36

    Clairvoyant Dreams 36

    Creative/Inspirational Dreams 37

    Scientific Dreams 37

    Repetitive Dreams 38

    Lucid Dreams 38

    Out of Body Experience Dreams (O.B.E.) 38

    Compensatory Dreams 38

Summary 39

Dream Catching 41

    Get a Good Night's Sleep 41

    Write It Down! 44

Summary 49

Dream Incubation 51

How to Incubate 52

    Step 1. Petition – Ask for a Dream 53

    Step 2. Ritual – Saturate the Mind with Expectancy 55

    Step 3. Report – Catch the Dream 57

    Step 4. Interpret – Find the Hidden Meaning 57

Summary 58

Dream Journaling *59*

How to Record Your Dreams 60

LongHand 60
Double Space 61
Present Tense 61
Feelings & Emotions 62
72-Hour Clause 62
Working Title 63
Details, Details, Details 64

Summary 66

The ABCs of Dream Healing *67*

What's in Your Closet? 69

A = "All That I See" 70

Summary 72

The Dream Walk *73*

Step 1: Identify Character, Object, Action 74
Step 2: Quality, Function, Feeling 75
Step 3: Dream Walk 81
Lenore's Asylum 84

What did you discover? 85

Summary 87

The Inquiry Method *89*

B = Become 90

Getting Started 91

Summary 93

Alien Interview *95*

Summary 97

- Six "Magic" Questions 97

Dream Coaching **99**

- **There's Rules!** 101
- **Laser Dream Coaching Protocol** 103
  - Step 1: A = All That I See 103
  - Step 2: Choose a Scene 104
  - Step 3: Associate into the Scene 104
  - Step 4: B = Become 106
  - Step 5: The Inquiry Method 107
  - Step 6: Alien Interview 108
  - Step 7: C = Connect 109
  - Step 8: C = Commit 109
- **Summary** 110

The Aesthetic Experience 113

- **The Felt Sense** 113
  - Muscle Response Test (MRT) 115
  - Body Sway Test 117
- **An Oracle** 118
- **Summary** 119

Notice 121

- Associations 125
- Feelings and Emotions 125
- Exaggeration 125
- Patterns 125
- Contrast or Similarities 126
- Metaphors 126
- Surprise! 126

Art of Dream Healing 127

- **Story Boarding** 127

The Push Process 129
    Getting Started 130
    Push Processing 134
    Story Boarding 136

Summary 139

"This" Dream 141

    "All that I see . . ." 142
        Getting Started 144

Regression Hypnotherapy 147
    A = All That I See 149
    B = Become 151
    C = Connect 152
    C = Commit...153

That's All Folks!..157

Suggested Reading...160

Wendie Webber 162

The Devil's Therapy Series 163

I'll let you be in my dreams if I can be in yours.
~ **Bob Dylan,** Lyrics: 2001

Why Read This Book

If you are a dreamer, come in,
If you are a dreamer, a wisher, a liar,
A hop-er, a pray-er, a magic-bean-buyer . . .
If you're a pretender, come sit by my fire
For we have some flax-golden tales to spin.
Come in!
Come in![1]

Why is it that some people have a prolific and rich dream life while others languish in the desert of waking consciousness? It seems to have to do with attention. The reason too many people have little to no dream recall is that they don't pay attention to their dreams. Start paying attention to your dreams and you'll start to dream more.

Most people don't understand their dreams because dreams are often cryptic. This is because they reflect what we are not allowing into consciousness. Using symbolic language, they reveal something that the conscious mind didn't have time to deal with, doesn't know how to fix, or doesn't want to look at. Are you paying attention?

---

[1] *Where the Sidewalk Ends* by Shel Silverstein

I'm very passionate about dreams. I started paying attention to my dreams in my teens. I knew they were important. I just didn't know what they meant! In my mid-twenties, I had a very vivid dream in which a five-year-old gave me a warning. I had no idea how to interpret it. Following the recommendation of a friend, I went to a psychic. She didn't know anything about dreams, either.

It took me years to finally understand what my dream had been trying to tell me. I didn't have the tools back then. The tools you will discover in this book are the by-product of working with my own dreams for over thirty-five years. These are the methods that worked for me. I have taught them to others, and they worked for them, too, often in surprising ways. They can work for you, too.

Dream Healing is a self-healing, self-empowerment process you can do for yourself. It's a way to consult with your innermost self to receive answers to questions and solutions to problems. Dream Healing is for everyone. But if you're a healing practitioner, you need a way to get clear and stay clear so that you can show up more fully for your clients. Dream Healing gives you a way to do your own work of self-healing.

The Tools of Dream Healing Include:
1. Dream Catching
2. Dream Incubation
3. Dream Journaling
4. The ABCs of Dream Healing
5. The Dream Walk
6. The Inquiry Method
7. The Alien Interview
8. Dream Coaching Rules
9. The Aesthetic Experience
10. Push Process
11. Story Boarding Technique

Are you a hypnosis practitioner?

I have been a hypnosis practitioner specializing in regression-to-cause therapeutic hypnosis since 2000. But it wasn't until I attended my first Regression Hypnotherapy Boot Camp in 2009 that I realized the important connection between dreams and hypnosis. And it was all because of the gift of a question. During one of the breaks, we were discussing what we were learning, and someone asked me, "Wendie, how come you get this stuff?" I honestly didn't have an answer. I thought, *Doesn't everybody get this stuff?* After sleeping on it, the answer came to me. Dreams speak the language of the subconscious mind. That's where we work!

Working with my own dreams has taught me how to listen to the subconscious mind and honor what it has to say. It has taught me how to translate the native language of the subconscious mind into language the conscious mind can understand. It has also helped me to get comfortable navigating the subconscious mind and feel fearless in facilitating regression sessions. Dream work helped me to develop skills that are important to regression hypnotherapy, for example, observation skills, uncovering skills, and skill working with Parts. It has also taught me to cultivate an attitude of objectivity in sessions with clients. Dream Healing crosses over to regression techniques such as:

- Regression to a Past Event
- The Uncovering Procedure
- Inner Child Work
- Dialogue Work
- Emotional-Release Work
- Resourcing Techniques
- Insight Generating
- More . . .

What you will discover is that dream work is fun. This doesn't mean that you should take your dreams lightly, however. Dreams don't tell us what we already know. They show us what our conscious, thinking mind doesn't know, can't fix, or doesn't want to look at. For a hypnosis practitioner, this is valuable information! If you're a hypnosis practitioner, Dream Healing gives you a way to get familiar with the territory of your subconscious mind and get fluent in the language of the subconscious.

Dream Healing is a practice of listening and paying attention to what your subconscious mind has to say -- not telling it what to do. Your dreams will show you what your subconscious mind feels is important. As you work with your own dreams, you'll begin to develop a sixth sense for recognizing patterns and themes. This ability can help you immensely in your sessions with clients.

Most of us have friends and family members we'd love to help, but it may not be appropriate for you to do hypnotherapy with them. They may not feel comfortable diving into deeply personal material, and *you* may not want to go there, either. Dream Healing gives you a way to work with these folks and help them to find their own answers and solutions.

Hypnotherapy Is Dream Healing

Hypnotherapy is Dream Healing. We're helping a person to heal the underlying perceptions that contribute to the problems they come to see us about. We are not in the business of dealing with "facts." We're in the business of dealing with perceptions—both true and false. Those perceptions don't come out of nowhere. They are contained in past experiences, which are held in memory. Dream Healing allows you to view a person's history as a dream. As a result, you can relax, sit back, and take more of an observer role in your sessions. The father of psychotherapy, Sigmund Freud, recognized this. In fact, he called dreams "the Royal Road" to the unconscious.

This is what Dream Healing gives you—a path to the subconscious mind. Because hypnotherapy follows psychotherapy, Dream Healing gives you a way to work with your own subconscious mind in a way that matches what you do in hypnotherapy sessions with clients.

Dream Healing can make you a better hypnotherapist! As you work with your own dreams, you will be developing a skill that is unique to you, and that will empower you in your sessions with clients. Mastering these simple techniques will help you to develop your skill and confidence in your hypnotherapy sessions. The secret, really, is to get out of the way, stay curious, and let the subconscious mind *show* you. When you can sit back, relax, and let the client do all the work, not only will you feel more confident facilitating the healing process, your sessions will rock!

What You Will Learn

Dream work is all about you. It's about working with your subconscious mind and developing a relationship with your innermost self. Through the process of working with your own dreams, you will develop a deeper relationship with your subconscious mind.

You'll learn how to:

- Petition your dreams to receive guidance
- Catch your dreams
- Record your dreams

- Interpret your dreams
- Know when you have successfully interpreted a dream.

Dream Healing is for everyone. Dream Healing is fun! If you're a hypnosis practitioner, Dream Healing can give you the solid foundation you need to feel confident in your sessions with clients. This is the same system that helped me to understand how healing happens. It can help you to hone your skills as a healing practitioner. For example, you will learn how to:

- Make the client do the work.
- Identify the underlying aspects contributing to the client's issue.
- Open a dialogue with the client's subconscious mind.
- Know what questions to ask when you're interviewing a Part.
- Recognize how regression happens and what to do when it does happen.

Dream Healing is a skill that everybody should learn. I think you should learn it, too. I want you to get fired up about your dreams and discover for yourself how giving attention to your dream life can support you in your daily life.

So, come . . . sit by the fire . . . and let's dream together . . .

Why Dreams?

We all sleep. There's ample science to show that dreaming is just as important as sleep (and we all know how important sleep is.) You may not always remember your dreams, but every night, whether you realize it or not, you have five to seven dreams. That's approximately 2,200 dreams per year. By the time you reach the ripe old age of 70, you'll have had over 150,000 dreams! Clearly, something is going on here. The question is, "What?" We spend about a third of our life sleeping and dreaming. That's at least as much time as we spend working. If our work-life deserves so much attention, why not our dream life?

When we sleep, we dream.

Sleeping and dreaming are linked to learning and the repair of both the body and mind. Sleep is when the body works on physical maintenance and repairs. Dreaming is when learning and memory consolidation takes place. Dreaming is one of the ways the subconscious mind sorts through all the unprocessed psychological debris of the day. All the stuff the conscious mind didn't have time to deal with (or didn't want to deal with) is being processed while we sleep. If you're sleep-deprived, you're going to be dream-deprived.

Sleep is the reset button on the mind-body system. Sleep supports healthy cognitive and physical function. Dreaming is the subconscious mind working on the undigested bits of experience from the day. If you're sleep-deprived, you're going to be dream-deprived. That's a problem. If you're sleep-deprived, you're not releasing the unprocessed emotions of the day. As a result, the pressure builds up inside. That's stress. When the internal pressure becomes too great, it can generate symptoms.

Anxiety disorders are often related to sleep issues. According to sleep expert Dr. Rubin Naiman, "Sleep-disorders are the most prevalent health concern in America and probably the rest of the industrialized world today." The average person is getting less than seven hours of sleep a night. Some people are getting significantly less than that. It has been estimated that nearly 95 percent of all visits to primary health-care professionals are for stress-related issues. And sleep deprivation is one of the biggest problems of modern-day living, contributing to the stress load. Stressing the body-mind with not-enough sleep or too many toxins -- physically or emotionally -- depletes energy. This blocks the flow of natural healing energies. Healing requires energy. When there's not enough energy to do all the necessary repairs, symptoms appear physically or emotionally. Research shows a strong correlation between insufficient sleep and:

- Cardiovascular disease
- Stroke
- High blood pressure
- Heart attack
- Metabolic disorders
- Obesity
- Immune function

We are a sleep-deprived society. A survey conducted by the National Sleep Foundation found that 75 percent of American adults experience symptoms of sleep disorders at least a few nights per week. Millions of people are struggling with a chronic lack of sleep. Research shows that a person who averages five to six hours of sleep per night has a 50% increased risk for viral infections. Insufficient sleep has been linked to metabolic disorders and increases in cancer. A number of studies have linked the loss of deep sleep to the obesity epidemic. It's very difficult to manage your weight if you're not getting enough sleep.

Sleep-loss triggers the pre-diabetic condition, insulin resistance. Apparently, the chemical messengers that signal sleepiness overlap with the signals that trigger hunger. As a result, we can mistake being sleepy for being hungry! Apparently, women tend to make this mistake more than men. Being more rested will help to put you more in control of your choices, and you'll be less likely to mistake fatigue for hunger.

Sleep deprivation makes everything worse. If you're a healing practitioner, helping your clients improve their sleep can be a good place to begin a healing program because sleep deprivation is often a major contributor to their presenting problem. Millions of people struggle with chronic lack of sleep, difficulty falling asleep, problems staying asleep, and sleep-related breathing disorders. About 85 percent of people with depression have insomnia. The other 15 percent suffer from hypersomnia, which means they're long-sleepers. In both cases, depression is associated with compromised sleep. Evidence suggests that we're actually dreaming less. There are many reasons for this, but it's possible that depressed people may, in fact, be dreaming less. Dr. Naiman recommends that part of treatment should be to encourage dreaming. If you're a hypnosis practitioner, you can do this very easily!

The most common sleep problem is insomnia. Insomnia is the inability to get to sleep or stay asleep. Literally, millions of people suffer from insomnia. This makes for a big market for pharmaceuticals. Pills don't work as well as people believe. A recent study on prescription sleeping drugs confirmed this. For example, Trazodone was shown to work equally as well as a placebo, only without all the nasty side effects like heart problems and weight gain. In general, what sleep medications do is decrease the amount of time it takes to fall asleep—by about 10 – 15 minutes maximum. They do increase the total amount of sleep, but only by about 20 minutes. A side effect of sleep medications is that they tend to cause amnesia for night-time awakening. The sleep-deprived pill-popper is still waking up during the night. They just don't remember. They think they're getting a solid night's sleep when, in fact, they're not.

A lot of substances and medications suppress both sleep and dreaming. Anti-anxiety medications suppress deep sleep and rapid eye movement (REM) sleep. And yet these chemicals are often prescribed as sleeping pills. Antidepressant medications have been shown to do more harm than good. They disrupt the body-mind's natural ebb and flow by increasing serotonin levels in a relentless way. Elevated serotonin levels at night suppress sleep.

Eighty percent of people suffering from a mental health problem also suffer from insomnia. Virtually all depressed people have some sort of sleep disorder. In fact, insomnia is a classic symptom of depression. What's interesting is that science has confirmed that insomnia is actually a cause of depression!

Mind and body do not function independently. Sleep-deprivation negatively impacts our judgment, perception, and performance. It's responsible for the decline of both the quality and quantity of work produced on the job as well as the serious rise in accidents in the workplace. Even a little bit of sleep-loss affects cognition, which is a major contributor to motor vehicle accidents which contributes to chronic pain and depression.

An hour's sleep-loss may not seem like much, but sleep-deprivation has an accumulative effect on a person's cognitive abilities. It's not like you can't stay up late from time to time. Your mind-body system knows how to play catch-up. The problem is that most people don't get caught up on their sleep. They're chronically making withdrawals from the energy reserves meant for maintaining physical, cognitive, and psychological well-being.

Replacing a sleep-deficit isn't something you have to do all at once. An extra 15 minutes of sleep each night will take four nights to recover one hour of sleep. Do the math. If you're dealing with a chronic sleep-deficit over a number of years, it may take some time to recover those lost ZZZs, but it's do-able.

How much sleep?

Sleep-deprivation contributes to a host of other issues, and if you want to consult your dreams, you need to get enough sleep. The amount of sleep each of us needs varies, but on average, adults need a minimum of seven and a half hours to take care of the physical and psychological repairs that happen during sleep. As a result, some people are going to need more sleep.

Newborns need more sleep because they're growing fast. Teenagers tend to sleep more because there's a physical growth spurt that happens at puberty. The body is calling for more energy resources to support physical growth. Sleeping provides this energy. Also, teenagers are developing a sense of independence. Hormone changes can stir up psychological conflicts, which puts a bigger drain on their emotional energy resources. Dreaming provides the energy needed for conflict resolution. As we grow older, we need less sleep. This is primarily because, as we get older, parts of the body are no longer getting repaired.

The body needs sleep to regenerate. If you're dealing with an illness, you're going to need more sleep to allow the body to repair itself. This is why you're advised to rest and drink more fluids when you're fighting off a virus. If you're struggling with an emotional issue, you're going to need more dream time to sort through the psychological conflicts. For example, a person with depression needs more sleep because there's a drain on their emotional reserves. They need to dream more to sort through all the psychological debris.

Why seven and a half hours? It has to do with sleep cycles. There are five stages of sleep that we cycle through repeatedly each night. Each cycle lasts between 90 – 120 minutes, so we usually cycle through four or five times each night. (Babies and elderly cycle every 60 minutes.) A "good night's sleep" consists of five of these cycles. Five cycles of 90 minutes equals seven and a half hours. Each cycle tends to take you a little deeper than the previous cycle. The more cycles you can get in each night, the more restorative sleep you'll enjoy and the better you'll feel.

Sleep cycles

The first three stages only last about 20 minutes. Stage one is light sleep. As muscle activity slows down, you may experience occasional muscle twitching. During stage two, breathing and heart rate slow, and body temperature decreases slightly. Stage three is where deep sleep begins; the brain begins to produce slow delta waves. Stage four is very deep sleep occurs. During this state, breathing becomes very rhythmic, and there is very little muscle activity.

Without sufficient delta sleep, one can suffer from sleep deprivation. That's a problem. Stage four is deep, restorative sleep, during which regeneration and cell renewal occur. During deep sleep, the mind-body system geta a much-needed rest. This is the sleep we need to heal.

When you're falling asleep, you pass through a semi-permeable barrier called the "hypnogogic" state. Hypnogogic refers to the onset of sleep; the transitional phase between awake and sleep. When you're waking, it's called the "hypnopompic" state. Hypnopompic refers to the onset of wakefulness; the transitional phase between being asleep and being fully awake. First, you drift down through stages one, two, three, and four -- from light sleep to deep sleep and very deep sleep. Then, brainwave patterns gradually speed up as the whole cycle is reversed. You begin to move back up from stage four to stage three, back into stage two. Then, instead of returning to stage one and emerging from sleep, you go into stage five sleep which is just below the threshold between waking and sleeping. This initiates the next sleep cycle.

Stage five is REM sleep. REM stands for Rapid Eye Movement. If you watch a person when they're sleeping in stage five, you will see their eyes flitting back and forth. In this stage, you can have very visual dreams. For example, lucid dreams are REM dreams. REM sleep stimulates parts of the brain that are used for learning. As a result, this stage of sleep resembles being awake.

Each REM cycle is a little longer than the previous cycle, with the last REM cycle before waking being the longest. These are the dreams we tend to wake up with and can be like full-length movies. Most dreams occur during REM sleep. You can dream in other stages of sleep, but non-REM (NREM) dreams tend to be shorter and more shadowy. REM dreams are the ones we remember because they're visually vivid and full of action.

Why do we dream?

Dreams are critical to our health and vitality. When we go to sleep, the conscious mind goes into abeyance, and the subconscious mind goes to work sorting through the events of the day—solving problems, resolving conflicts, and consolidating learning into long-term memory.

Your dreams are about you. My dreams are about me. All dreams are meant to help and guide you on your path in life. They can help you to be happier and more successful in your relationships, work life, and daily living by showing us what the subconscious mind is working on, and feels is important.

The conscious mind is limited. It can only process about forty bits of information per second. The subconscious mind, on the other hand, can apparently process 20,000,000 bits of information per second. That's 500,000 times more information than the conscious mind is capable of handling. Now, I'm not sure who came up with these numbers, but it's evident that we're not able to process everything that's happening *consciously*. The conscious mind tends to get overwhelmed by too much information. This is the stuff that gets carried over to be worked on while we sleep.

The contents of our dreams are the stuff of our waking life and can point to internal conflicts, unresolved fears, and inadequacies. They can show you unfulfilled desires and blocks to performance.

Sometimes, our dreams reflect issues of identity. They can point to relationship concerns or a search for purpose. Sometimes, they're repetitive in order to get our attention. Are you listening?

What is a dream?

A dream is subconscious communication in the form of a story. It's a story you tell yourself, about yourself, in the privacy of your own mind. And it's all about you.

According to the Online Dictionary, dreams are:

1) A succession of images, thoughts, or emotions passing through the mind during sleep.
2) An involuntary vision occurring to a person when awake.

The shamanic perspective suggests three kinds of dreams. They are:

1) Night dreams
2) Day dreams
3) *This* dream

The methods described in this book can be applied equally to all three types of dream because the language of your innermost mind is image and emotion. The subconscious mind makes no distinction between real and imagined.

This Dream

Have you ever had a nightmare where you woke up in a sweat with your heart pounding? A dream can seem very real because what makes anything real is how it feels. Dreams reflect daily issues. The contents of our dreams have their roots in actual experiences in waking life.

Whether it's a day dream, a night dream, or "this" dream, as far as your subconscious mind is concerned, it's a real event. As such, any emotional event in daily life can reveal hidden meaning when viewed as a dream.

Day Dream

A day dream or waking dream is when the conscious mind takes a little time out. This happens naturally during the Basic Rest Activity Cycle (BRAC). Throughout the day, the body-mind system needs to take a little break. This happens approximately every 90 – 120 minutes. For about 20 minutes, the conscious mind wanders off, and you get caught up in a daydream. If you've ever zoned-out while driving the car and missed your turn on the freeway, you know what I'm talking about! These spontaneous day dreams can be interpreted.

Night Dream

Night dreams are those spontaneously-occurring nocturnal movies we all experience. The benefit of working with a night dream is that, unlike a day dream or this dream, there is no conscious mind interference. This makes a night dream pure, unadulterated subconscious communication. That's something worth paying attention to. With practice, you'll be able to recall one, two, or three dreams every morning if you want to.

What equipment do you need?

Dream work doesn't require any special equipment. Don't bother with the fancy-pants, expensive leather-bound journals. Your dream journal is really a workbook for exploring your inner life. You'll be making notes in the margins and drawing pictures. It's going to get messy.

All you really need is a notepad next to your bed and a spiral-bound, 350-page subject notebook for the interpretation process. Highlighters and colored pens are optional. If you're a dedicated dream worker, you're going to go through a lot of journals. Stock up when the back-to-school sales come on. You know you're going to use them! The 8 ½ X 11 size fits nicely into a standard file storage box. Notate the start-date and end-date on the front of each scribbler before filing them away. That way, if you need to, you'll be able to find a specific journal easily. (I have gone back 15 years to find a dream!)

I have a favorite room I like to journal in. I have my favorite chair and a place to put my morning coffee. My notebook sits on my lap. That's another benefit of using a spiral-bound scribbler; you can fold the pages back so that your journal lays flat. This means you can work on your dreams anywhere -- in bed, in the waiting room at the doctor's office, while commuting by train or boat, or in a sacred place you create for inner work.

Summary

Both sleeping and dreaming are therapeutic. While we sleep, the body works on physical repairs and maintenance. While we dream, the mind works on emotional healing and learning consolidation. The first step to remembering your dreams is to get enough sleep. If you're not getting enough sleep, you'll be over-tired. If you're over-tired, you won't remember your dreams. How much sleep? Five sleep cycles. That means a minimum of seven and a half hours.

Sleep-deprivation is a serious problem for a good many people and is strongly correlated with a host of physical and psychological health concerns. The most common sleep problem is insomnia. Not being able to get to sleep or stay asleep negatively impacts cognition and performance. It's a major contributor to accidents behind the wheel and in the workplace. Research indicates that it may, in fact, be the cause of depression. While an hour's sleep-loss may not seem like much, sleep-deprivation has an accumulative effect. The mind-body system knows how to play catch-up, but most people don't take action to catch up on their sleep. As a result, their energy reserves are chronically deficient.

If you're sleep-deprived, you're dream-deprived. You need to pass through stage four sleep to get to stage five sleep. Stage four is deep, restorative sleep, which allows physical healing. Stage five is where we dream in living color. REM dreams are memorable dreams! When you wake, you'll wake up with a story!

A Brief History

Ancient peoples paid attention to their dreams. In modern times, the tendency is to view dreams as "woo-woo[2]." But every culture throughout the world has a tradition that honors their dreams. Cross-culturally, dreams have been consulted for the purposes of healing and guidance. If you think about it, it makes sense. Before the invention of electricity, when it got dark, people went to bed and woke up at daybreak. They probably got better quality sleep than we do in modern life and were more in tune with nature. As a result, their inner and outer lives were more in sync.

Cultures that have traditionally honored their dreams include Hindu, Japanese, Muslim, Hawaiian Kahuna, and Australian Aboriginal traditions. Shamanic traditions employed the use of trance states through ecstatic body postures, trance dance, chanting, and drumming. Shamanic journeys were then taken for the purposes of healing, spirit releasement therapy, and soul retrieval.

Babylonians

Over 4,500 years ago, the Babylonians of ancient Mesopotamia kept close tabs on their dream life. They believed that we have good dreams and bad dreams. The priests who served the goddess of dreams,

---

[2] Woo-woo is defined as unconventional beliefs regarded as having little or no scientific basis, especially those relating to spirituality, mysticism or alternative medicine.

Mamu, had the same job as your subconscious Mamu—to make sure that bad dreams didn't come true. The Assyrians who conquered Babylon also believed in good dreams and bad dreams. But they believed that dreams were omens. They believed the way to get rid of a bad dream was to understand it and then act on it.

Egyptians

Archeological finds show that the Egyptians were the first to record their dreams. Dream records written on papyrus have been found dating as far back as 2000 BC. The Egyptians honored their dreams because they believed that dreams were messages from the gods. They believed the contents of dreams were based on real things that were not visible to the conscious mind. Dreams fell under one of three categories. (1) Dreams in which the gods show themselves, often demanding some pious act. (2) Dreams containing revelations or warnings (perhaps about illness). (3) Dreams invoked through ritual, usually in a healing temple.

Dreams were an important part of life for the ancient Egyptians and were considered a valuable source of healing and guidance. Temples and shrines were established and dedicated to dream healing. Ancient civilizations did not separate science and religion because they saw no separation between material and spiritual realities. One was equally as valid as the other. The gods were real and played an active part in daily life.

Shrines and sanctuaries were attended by priest-physicians who acted as healing guides during a nine-day sleep treatment. Dream incubation[3] was practiced to petition the gods to provide answers or healing

---

[3] Incubate comes from the Latin *incubare*, which means "to lie down."

prescriptions. Rituals, purification rites, prayers, and sacrificial offerings to the gods helped to invoke feelings of awe before sleep. The gods were called upon to reveal a solution to the problem, or issue, calling for healing. The patient would then "sleep on it: and in the morning, the priest-physician would listen to the patient's dream and prescribe a healing solution. The dream provided the basis for prescription! The forms of treatment commonly used included sympathetic magic[4] and amulets. In some cases, especially when the god appeared in the dream, the dream itself was the healing.

Sympathetic magic involved the use of words and rituals to heighten the client's expectation that something would happen. Today, we call this the power of suggestion. Amulets were objects with symbolic meaning that were charged with the power of magical words. These objects acted as symbolic reminders to encourage the desired change. What the ancient physicians called "magic" is recognized today as the basis of placebo and nocebo -- the power of belief!

Magic requires authority. White magic has a positive intent. It is meant to do good, be helpful, empower, and heal. Black magic, on the other hand, is used to control and do harm.

First, do no harm. - Hippocrates

Because life in Egypt was dependent upon the black, fertile soil of the Nile, it was originally known as the land of "Khem." the Egyptian word for "black." Some scholars believe that ancient Egypt is where the science of alchemy began. Alchemy is a form of ancient chemistry. Where modern chemistry deals with the empirical realm, alchemy is a

---

[4] Magic based on the assumption that a person or thing can be supernaturally affected through its name or an object representing it

spiritual process. Its purpose is to reveal the underlying essence of all things. often referred to as "the beauty of All Beauty," "the love of All Love," and "the High Most High." This Highest or Divine Order is the goal of alchemy. The philosophers of old sought to discover the elixir of immortality through the transmutation of base metals (lead) into gold. The ancient alchemist writings make clear, however, that the substance of transmutation was not literally lead but the human soul.

The name alchemy reflects this theme of transmutation, for example, "Alkamye" from the Old French, "Alchimia" from Medieval Latin, Arabic "Al kimiya" (meaning the transmutation), and the Late Greek "khemeia" (meaning the art of transmutation).

> *Alchemy pertains to the hidden reality of the highest order which constitutes the underlying essence of all truths and all religions.*
> ~ **Stanislas Klossowski de Rola**

Alchemy could be called *the Transmutation of Perception*. It is a process of changing one's perception by transmuting the ordinary, lead-like, material level of perception to the level of perceiving the gold-like perfection of the "highest order" in everything. In other words, seeing the Divine in everything. Carl Jung, who dialogued and received guidance through an inner guide named Phaedrus, suggested that the vehicles of this transformative process were archetypes: inherited patterns of thought or symbolic images that were present in the individual's unconscious with roots in the past collective experience.

Archetypes are internal representations (symbols) that transcend personal meaning. They are a global, cross-cultural language we all share. Examples of archetypes include: The Wise Man/Woman; Inner

Child; Mother/Father; Fool; Water; Sun; Moon; Stars; King/Queen; Warrior; Inner Guides, (which would be the equivalent of the ancient gods, angels, Higher Self, Holy Spirit), and the devil (of course.)

Greeks

The Ancient Greeks loved everything Egyptian. They adopted many Egyptian customs, including the establishment of sleep temples. These were the original Dream Healing centers where dream incubation was the leading edge in the healing arts of the day. The most famous is the Temple of Epidaurus, established by the Greek healer Asclepius during the early 4th century BC. The staff of Asclepius has a snake twining around it. This symbol was adopted by modern medicine for a good reason. Asclepius was a serious healer who achieved status as a god of medicine. The archives discovered in the Temple of Epidaurus contain over 100,000 documented healings.

Many of the ancient Greek gods had their equivalents in the Egyptian pantheon of gods. For example, the Greek god Hermes corresponded with the Egyptian god Thoth. Both were gods of writing and magic, as well as guides to the afterlife. Asclepius was a real person, but his reputation for healing the sick through dreams eventually raised him to the status of a god. As a result, he is known both as a physician and as a god. Like the Egyptians, the Greeks believed that dreams were sent in the service of healing. Either the dream *was* the healing, as indicated by the presence of the god, or the dream offered instruction as the basis of prescription!

Romans

The practice of sleep temples naturally spread to Rome. They, too, took their dreams very seriously. They believed the gods made their presence known through dreams. So strongly did they believe that it was necessary to find out the wishes of the god that Emperor Augustus, grand-nephew of Julius Caesar, ruled that anyone who had a dream about the state must proclaim it in the marketplace.

In the 2nd Century AD, a diviner of dreams named Artemidorus traveled the known world learning cross-cultural dream interpretation techniques. He wrote down all he learned from Greek, Roman, Assyrian, and Egyptian records into five comprehensive volumes, which he called the Oneirocritica (Interpreter of Dreams). Dreams were considered so important that this book was used as an authoritative source by authors up to the 18th Century.

> *For God speaketh once, yea twice, yet man perceiveth it not. In a dream, in a vision of the night when deep sleep falleth upon men slumbering upon their bed, then He openeth their ears and sealeth in their instructions.*
> ~ Job 33:14 - 16

Hebrews

The Hebrews also incubated to receive dreams. They believed in good dreams and bad dreams. Good dreams were divine revelation or the "voice of god." Bad dreams came from evil spirits. The above quote from the Book of Job suggests that God repeatedly speaks to us directly through dreams. When we sleep, our conscious mind goes into abeyance, leaving us open to listening to His instructions. These experiences are real experiences that are "sealed" in our memory. The problem is that we either don't pay attention to our dreams, or we fail to understand the messages conveyed by them.

Joseph was a Hebrew slave who healed two nations by correctly interpreting a dream. Joseph began life as the baby of the family. He became the favorite son of his father, Jacob (who became known as Israel.) This favoritism didn't make him popular with his significantly older brothers. They tolerated the boy. But when Joseph made the mistake of sharing a dream which revealed that he would rise above his brothers in stature, that did it! Their resentment became a plot to do away with the boy. Fortunately, at the last minute, they had a change of heart, and instead of murdering the boy, they sold him to a passing caravan of slave traders on the way to Egypt.

In Egypt, Joseph served as a houseboy for the warden of the prison. We'll probably never know the full story, but Joseph ends up in prison for two years, during which time he develops his skill as a dream healer. Two of his cellmates are palace servants -- the king's cupbearer and baker. Joseph accurately interprets their dreams which foretells their release from prison. As a result, when Pharaoh is visited by a disturbing and recurring dream which his magicians are unable to interpret, Joseph is sent for. Joseph is brought before Pharoah, and Pharaoh shares his dream.

In the dream, Pharaoh witnesses seven fat cows being followed by seven lean cows. Joseph interprets this dream to mean that there will be seven years of plenty followed by seven years of famine. Based on this interpretation, Joseph recommends that Pharaoh order grain to be stored up during the years of plenty -- just in case.

Sure enough, Pharaoh's dream proved to be prophetic. When famine struck, Joseph's dream working skills saved Egypt. In fact, there was such a surplus of grain that Egypt was able to make a tidy profit trading with other countries that were unprepared for food shortages.

Joseph's skill as a diviner of dreams brought him status. He was elevated from the position of slave to Vizier, akin to being Prime Minister. In other words, he was second only to the King! Just as foretold in the dream which had landed him in Egypt in the first place, Joseph did, indeed, rise above his brothers!

Not only did he save his adopted country from hard times, but he was also placed in a position where he could save his own family by bringing them down to Egypt to join him. Joseph forgave his brothers, and gave them fertile lands and livestock. And the rest is history.

Unlike today, the prophets of the Old Testament were respected for their ability to receive guidance through dreams which could be prophetic and served the following four important purposes:

1. To act as a warning to avoid or refrain from a considered course of action
2. To guide the dreamer away from pride and keep him humble
3. To steer the dreamer away from a path of sinfulness or disbelief in God
4. To protect the dreamer from an untimely or violent death

Hawaiian

Where Jung believed dreams were attempts at problem-solving, the Hawaiian Kahunas (meaning priest, sorcerer, magician, wizard, minister, or expert in any profession) believed the dreams, themselves, could solve problems and bring about healing. They believed that the miracle of healing was achievable by anyone provided they had faith, were free of guilt, could imagine the desired result (i.e., healing), and were able to make telepathic contact with the spiritual realm through their higher self.

Australian

The Australian Aboriginal creation myth centers around the "Dreamtime," an ancient time when spirits, who had been sleeping underground, arose and wandered across the earth, singing the names of everything and shaping the landscape. They made humans and taught them the art of survival before returning underground to sleep once again. In many ways, the Australian creation myth matches the Hebrew creation myth in which God brought forth creation through a series of "utterances."

Native American

Native American Indians believed dreams reveal the hidden wishes of the soul. The most vivid dreamer was chosen as medicine man. The origins of psychodrama lie with the Iroquois, who tried to make their desires come true by acting them out.

Acting out a bad dream could facilitate problem-solving. For example, if the dream revealed defeat in battle, acting it out allowed the tribe to discover a way to win -- based on the dream. Acting out a good dream would increase courage and positive expectancy of success for the whole tribe.

Virginia Satir's approach to Parts Therapy includes a technique called "sculpting" where a scene is set and acted out through vignettes. John and Helen Watkin's Ego State Therapy employs a dialoguing technique called the Empty Chair. Fritz Perl's Gestalt Therapy is a process of verbally acting out a dream using active imagination.

Summary

Ancient cultures took their dreams very seriously. They viewed dreaming as a divination tool and a path to healing. Today, dreams are viewed more psychologically as a mental process involving memory consolidation and self-healing.

Two Minds

Ashleigh Brilliant wrote, "The mind is a wonderful thing. Everyone should have one!" We all assume we *have* a mind, but what, exactly, is it? The ancient Greeks believed that we have two minds: a brain mind and a heart mind. The brain mind thinks. The heart mind feels.

Sigmund Freud's model gave us the conscious and unconscious mind. The conscious mind is the thinking mind. The unconscious (or subconscious) mind is the feeling mind. These two parts of us communicate very differently. The conscious mind is all about facts. It uses reason and logic to make sense of things, and analysis and logic to solve problems. It's also very linear. The past is "back there," and the future is "out there." The present is in the "here and now." The conscious mind is very useful when it comes to balancing the check book, making out grocery lists, and managing a schedule. But it's just the tip of the iceberg. Just below the surface lies the subconscious mind, sometimes referred to as the Heart Mind.

Our subconscious mind doesn't rely on words. It uses images, pictures, memories, and the feelings associated with those things to communicate. It doesn't think - it feels. This is because the subconscious mind is responsible for holding onto all our memories and what we learned from them. What makes anything memorable is how it feels! This makes this part of us significantly more influential than our conscious, thinking mind.

Where do we feel our feeling? In the body, right? According to psycho-neuro-immunologist Candace Pert, the *body* is the subconscious mind. Any event that makes an impression on the nervous system of the body gets stored for future reference as memory. It is this ability that has helped us survive as a species. Have you ever had a "bad dream" where you woke up sweating, breathing rapidly, with your heart pounding? In dreams, we see and feel and respond to the dream as if it were really happening. A dream can generate a real physiological response because, psychologically, a dream is an actual event.

Your subconscious mind makes no distinction between real and imagined. It will generate real emotions and real physiological changes based on your perception of the event. It doesn't matter whether it's a day dream, a night dream, or "this" dream. If it involves some kind of emotion, as far as your subconscious mind is concerned, what you are experiencing is an actual event. Because the subconscious mind makes no distinction between an event in waking life and a dream event, both are valid realities, which makes them valid opportunities for healing. If you're holding onto an unresolved issue from the past, situations in daily life can trigger the subconscious mind to reach down into your memory banks and pull out the file to work on it. That's when you'll have a dream. This is a healing process that occurs each and every night.

Zero Point Field is a theoretically vast, inexhaustible source of energy that is all around us. Similar to Carl Jung's Collective Unconscious, the Field is an invisible sea of energy connecting everything in the universe to everything else. Scientists are showing that what appears to be solid matter is actually a collection of energy charges called subatomic particles interacting with this Field. At the core of every particle of matter is a unique frequency signature communicating with the Field.

Recent research in the field of neuroscience has discovered something remarkable. The heart is not merely a pump, as was once believed, but is also a brain. The heart brain is in constant communication with the Field. The head brain, on the other hand, is merely a receiving and transmitting mechanism which selectively downloads information from the Field and uses it to create the images we see in front of us. Further, through our heart-connection to the Field, we influence one another with our thoughts and intentions (which may explain why phenomena such as remote viewing, distance healing, prayer, and vibrational healing have been shown to be successful.) The heart actually has its own independent nervous system with at least 40,000 neurons. Not only does it communicate with the Field, but it also communicates with the brain and the rest of the body. It does so through:

1) the transmission of nerve impulses
2) hormones and neurotransmitters
3) pressure waves
4) electromagnetic field interactions

The heart may actually be the intelligence behind intuitive thoughts and feelings as well as the primary source of emotions. This certainly adds new meaning to the age-old advice to "listen to your heart" and "follow your heart." When head and the heart are in agreement, we experience "flow" in life. We're in alignment and all that we see reflects it. We experience health, happiness, and harmony. When our thinking and feeling are in conflict, however, there's a problem. No matter what you think, when head and heart get into a tug of war, the conscious, thinking mind is no match for the power of imagination and emotions. That's the language of the subconscious mind -- the same language as dreams.

In every moment, you are broadcasting a very specific vibrational signal that is instantly being understood and answered ... and immediately your present and future circumstances begin changing in response to the signal you are projecting. The entire Universe, right now, is being affected by what you are offering. –
Abraham Hicks

Summary

The conscious mind, or brain mind, is the part of us that thinks. The subconscious mind, or heart mind, is the part of us that feels. These two parts of us function very differently. The body truly is the subconscious mind! Neuroscience has discovered that the heart is a brain with its own independent nervous system. The heart may actually be the intelligence behind intuition as well as the primary source of emotions.

The subconscious mind makes no distinction between real and imagined. As a result, a dream can generate real physiological responses. Situations in daily life can act as reminders of old, unresolved emotional issues from the past. This can trigger the subconscious mind to reach into the memory banks and generate a dream.

When head and heart are in harmony, we experience flow in life. When thinking and feeling are in conflict, there's a problem. Thinking is no match for the power of imagination and emotion -- the language of the subconscious mind. The same language as dreams.

A Dream Is a Story

Michelle woke with two dreams and immediately recognized that they were significant. Both dreams were telling the same story but in different ways. In the first dream, Michelle was renting a basement suite. In the second dream, she was living in her parent's basement. It was clear that her subconscious mind was looking for a solution to a problem by rehearsing different scenarios. Deciphering the dream showed Michelle where she was getting stuck. What was interesting was it revealed a pattern that was playing out in both her workplace and her personal relationships. Until she deciphered the dream, however, this was something that she was completely unaware of.

A dream is a story we tell ourselves *about ourselves* in the privacy of our own minds. Dreams show us what the conscious mind doesn't know, can't fix, or doesn't want to look at. The problem is that the conscious mind doesn't *have* the whole story. If you want to know what's really going on in your life, you need to consult your dreams. What Michelle's dreams revealed surprised her! It brought to light issues she hadn't even considered. It also raised uncomfortable questions. Upon reflection, Michelle realized that these were important questions, questions she needed to be asking in order to resolve the impasse in her life. This helped her to think very differently about her approach to situations in waking life.

Types of Dreams

There are many different types of dreams but basically three categories of dreams -- physiological dreams, psychological dreams and spiritual dreams.

Physiological dreams are physical. These are dreams that you feel in your body. e.g., dreams of falling, and night terrors, while more intense, physiological dreams lack content.

Psychological dreams are stories that play out like a movie. Like any story, they have a beginning, middle, and end. The dream narrative tells you about yourself. But it's seldom what you think because dreams don't tell us what we already know. They show us what we are not allowing into consciousness, what we don't want to look at, and unanswered questions or issues we're struggling to resolve. Dreams show us what's calling for healing, what your subconscious mind feels is important and is working on.

Spiritual dreams begin at the psychological level, but they have a deeper meaning. These dreams tell a story, too, but their point of reference is identity. Spiritual dreams deal with concepts like life purpose, calling in life, and your relationship to the Divine, whatever you perceive that to be. The great psychologist, Carl Jung, recognized the value of dreams for both psychological and spiritual development. He believed that they give us access to internal sources of wisdom that are not accessible to the conscious mind.

Venting Dreams

According to John Kappas, of the Hypnosis Motivation Institute, dreams which occur during the first 1 ½ - 2 hours of sleep are the least intense. They are usually concerned with clearing out surface stuff (not requiring processing). Whatever filled our perception last is likely to be dealt with during the first cycle. For example, if you watched CNN before bed, a news report that made an impression will likely produce a "garbage" dream. Reading something inspiring or focusing on a desired goal at bedtime, on the other hand, will likely produce pleasant "wish fulfillment dreams." The next 1 ½ - 2 hours are more concerned with sorting out life concepts or beliefs that govern our behavior. During this period, the subconscious mind is working on a puzzle, sorting out all the pieces of data and finding a way to make them fit. All the pieces are there, but the conscious mind hasn't been able to put them all together.

Problem-Solving Dreams

Dreams are often used for problem-solving. This is why it's always a good idea to "sleep on it" before making an important decision. Your dreams may provide help and guidance in the decision-making process. Whenever we see the pattern of the puzzle, we experience an "aha!" This genre of dreams is called "problem-solving" and can sometimes be precognitive. It's important to recognize that the answers provided by dreams reflect how things look right now. As more pieces are added and more information is provided, the picture changes. Once the puzzles are complete, the subconscious mind must make room for new ones. It does so by venting out energy through feelings and sensations. During this phase of dreaming, we can experience the releasing of old energies.

All dreams have a positive and healing purpose, even "bad dreams." "Bad" dreams may actually indicate the completion of an issue the subconscious mind has been working on. It's through the expression of negative feelings that the problem is released. Unfortunately, if the dreamer interprets a "venting dream" as precognitive, this effectively "re-installs" the negativity as a fearful expectation.

Nightmares

Nightmares reflect anxieties. When unresolved, these themes can carry over from childhood into adult life. e.g., anxieties due to criticism in childhood generate a dream in the adult of being on trial. Resolving the cause puts an end to reruns.

Factual Dreams

"Factual dreams" are logical dreams. They are usually simple, practical, and to the point. There's little to no symbolic significance, so they're fairly easy to understand. They tend to deal with daily, often trivial experiences, and the characters are all known to the dreamer. Factual dreams can serve to finish off the day's affairs or help to resolve past difficulties. Sometimes these dreams will incorporate environmental noise, such as a dripping faucet, passing traffic, a partner snoring, or a ticking clock to remind us of things we need to do. For example., if your bladder is full, you may have a dream that reminds you to get up and go to the toilet.

Clairvoyant Dreams

"Clairvoyant dreams" offer a glimpse into the future. They can be prophetic, frequently foretelling disaster. These dreams present knowledge the dreamer could not have acquired through normal means. There are two kinds of clairvoyant dreams: warning dreams and anxiety dreams. Warning dreams, which foretell disaster, seem to have to do with extra-sensory perception or paranormal abilities. They can also reflect deep fears and anxieties. Anxiety dreams are the result of clues being picked up unconsciously in waking life. They could also be the result of repressed fears triggered during waking hours.

Creative/Inspirational Dreams

Creative dreams can be a source of original ideas and inspiration. These dreams are often produced by having a relaxed mind after focusing on a problem. Both Thomas Edison and Albert Einstein routinely took catnaps while working on a problem. This would allow creative solutions to come to the surface.

Robert Louis Stevenson's character Mr. Hyde was inspired by a dream, as was Charles Dickens' *A Christmas Carol*, in which Scrooge is visited in a dream by three spirits. This timeless story is a commentary on both societal values and the transmutation of the soul from lead to gold (alchemy). It shows how dreams can change us!

Scientific Dreams

Scientists and mathematicians have found solutions through dreams. For example, the German chemist, Friedrich von Stradonitz, dreamt of a snake swallowing its own tail. This led to the discovery that the atoms of the benzene molecule are arranged in a circle and not in a straight line, as had once been believed. The movie, *Lorenzo's Oil*, tells the true story of a boy who suddenly loses muscular control and begins to have seizures. He enters a paralytic trance state and is diagnosed with a rare type of cerebral demyelination called adrenoleukodystrophy (ALD). There was no treatment for this condition, but Lorenzo's father, Augusto, refused to give up. He had no medical training, but he immersed himself in pouring over medical texts, searching day and night for the key to his son's healing. One night, Augusto fell asleep over his books in the library. And he had a dream. This dream eventually helped scientists to develop a treatment for ALD, which was based on canola oil. From this comes the term, "Lorenzo's oil."

Repetitive Dreams

Dreams can be repetitive or sequential. You can have different dreams which present a recurring theme, like searching for something, or you can have the same dream over several nights or even years. Sequential dreams are the subconscious equivalent of a television mini-series. Repetitive dreams show patterns or themes associated with unresolved issues.

Lucid Dreams

Lucid dreaming is when the dreamer is aware that she is dreaming. These dreams tend to occur most frequently in the early morning. Lucid dreams are REM dreams. In a lucid dream, the dreamer's senses are heightened, especially vision, and there is much greater awareness of detail. Lucid dreaming can be learned but it takes time and perseverance. With practice the dreamer can learn to control events. This can be very empowering as it enables wish-fulfillment, problem-solving, and the ability to address fears and anxieties.

Out of Body Experience Dreams (O.B.E.)

OBEs are similar to lucid dreams. They can occur during sleep, unconsciousness (for example, while under anesthesia), and during a near-death experience. During an OBE dream, the consciousness seems to leave the physical body. The physical self is often seen from outside the body and, in some cases, the dreamer has the ability to travel to more spiritual realms of existence.

Compensatory Dreams

Carl Jung believed that dreams can provide balance to the personality. Compensatory dreams help to counterbalance failings and needs by allowing the dreamer to see him/herself in a new and strange light. Such dreams often have content that is surprising to the dreamer. For example, a timid man who is too afraid to approach women dreams of having a harem. Compensatory dreams can be "safety valve" dreams which serve the purpose of releasing internal pressure and tension. By allowing a person to behave in unacceptable ways or express desires he may not be aware of, dreams may help to resolve deep, inner conflicts. For example, a kind person dreams of committing violence. Compensatory dreams can also be in response to extreme feelings during waking life. For example, experiencing overwhelming grief, intense happiness, or extreme excitement would be counterbalanced by the dream experience. In this case, the dream, itself, serves as the healing.

Summary

Dreams support our physical and emotional well-being. They can offer spiritual support by giving us access to states of consciousness and sources of wisdom that, normally, we have no awareness of in waking consciousness. There are many different kinds of dreams, but the most common category of dreams are physiological dreams, psychological dreams and spiritual dreams.

Dreams can give us a glimpse into the future or be consulted for new ideas and inspiration. Problem-solving dreams can provide answers to questions and solutions to problems. You can have recurring or repetitive dreams, lucid dreams where you're aware that you're dreaming, and out of body dreams. Compensatory dreams can help you to feel better about yourself by helping to bring more balance to the psyche.

Dreams are the touchstones of our characters.
~ **Henry David Thoreau**

Dream Catching

The first step to working with your dreams is to have one. This begins with making sure you're getting enough sleep. Sleep deprivation is a big problem in this country. Insufficient or poor-quality sleep makes any problem worse. Worse, there is strong evidence that people are dreaming less and less. Conditions like depression, which are associated with compromised sleep, may actually be caused by dream deprivation. You won't remember your dreams if you're over-tired. When you wake up, you want to feel refreshed. You also want to wake up with a dream.

Get a Good Night's Sleep

Sleep requires the right conditions. To fall asleep, you need to be able to relax. If you're stressed-out from a tough day, or you're feeling wired or jangled, you're going to have a hard time falling asleep. Your conscious mind needs time to wind down at the end of the day. If you've had a haywire day, you need to do something to de-stress before going to bed. Have a warm bath or do some light exercise before bed. Yoga is good. Self-hypnosis or meditation is a wonderful way to end the day. If you're a media addict, and you just have to watch the news, do it earlier in the day. At bedtime, you need to relax. Read something positive and uplifting or inspiring before sleep. Put that in last and your subconscious mind will process it and find a way to incorporate it into your memory banks.

To get a good night's sleep, your bedroom needs to be dark, quiet and warm – but not stuffy. Open a window a little to allow some fresh air in. This will help you to get the restorative sleep you need so you can wake up feeling refreshed. A lot of people don't realize this, but the brain needs total darkness to rest. Modern-day city living has created another problem on top of dream deprivation – darkness deprivation. There's evidence that ambient light can disrupt brain function. Make sure your bedroom is dark. If you're a city-dweller, you've got streetlights and city lights to contend with. It never really gets dark in the city. In some places, there's so much ambient light that you can't see the stars at night! That's sad. It's also a problem for your brain. You can get room-darkening drapes or blinds that are designed to block out ambient streetlight. This will help to encourage the restorative sleep you need. Another source of ambient light that can disrupt your sleep cycle is having an illuminated clock or night light in the bedroom. Cover it up! There's also evidence that WIFI signals can disrupt sleep cycles. Remove digital devices from the bedroom.

Remember, there are five stages to the sleep cycle. What happens during the first stage of sleep is that the body is slowing down and the muscles begin to relax. As this happens, there can be involuntary muscle twitches. This is a good thing! The body is releasing tension from the muscles – so you can sleep. In stage two, breathing and heart rate will slow down. As this happens, there will be a slight decrease in body temperature. Your room should be cool while your bed needs to be warm.

When you dream, the subconscious mind goes to work, sorting through all the pieces of the puzzle that the conscious mind hasn't been able to put together. All the pieces need to be sorted and cleared out to make room for new ones. The last thing you input will be processed first. This is when you're most likely to have venting dreams. If you wake from a bad dream, realize that what's probably happening is you're releasing negative emotions. That's good! You don't have to hold onto those feelings! Your subconscious mind is taking the garbage out!

In the third stage, you enter into deep sleep. It's here that the brain starts to generate those slow delta waves. As you drift down even deeper, you enter into stage four which is very deep sleep. This is the restorative sleep we all need for mind and body to regenerate. Drugs and alcohol can rob you of this restorative stage of sleep. This includes sleeping pills. Some prescription drugs can cause dreamless sleep. Others disrupt brain activity and can cause weird and disturbing dreams. The effects of drugs can be cumulative. If you've been prescribed certain medications and you're not sleeping well, or you're not waking feeling rested, talk to your doctor. You're not getting enough deep sleep to be healthy.

In stage five, your brain waves speed up, again, and this is when REM sleep occurs. This is when you're most likely to have a dream. If you wake with a vivid dream, you probably emerged from REM sleep. Dreaming gets progressively longer as we progress through the sleep cycles. The first REM dream of the night is usually about five minutes long. The last dream you have, just before waking, can be anywhere from 15 minutes to an hour long. These dreams can be epic movies and are the ones you're most likely to remember when you wake. Because we dream more toward the end of normal sleep, you want to be prepared to catch the dream as soon as you wake. Keep a pen and notepad next to your bed. That way, you'll be able to record your dream as soon as you wake up.

Write It Down!

Samuel Coleridge's poem, Kublai Khan, was also titled "A Vision in a Dream" and "A Fragment." According to Coleridge, he woke from a long and vivid dream and immediately set about writing lines of poetry that came to him from the dream. Unfortunately, before he could capture all the fantastic detail from his dream about a marvelous pleasure dome, he was called away for about an hour. When he returned to finish recording his dream, "All the rest had passed away like the images on the surface of a stream."

When we wake, we cross over the threshold between dreaming to waking consciousness. When you wake up with a dream, the biggest mistake you can make is to assume that you'll remember it. If you put off writing down your dream, there's a good chance you'll lose it. Recall during those initial moments of waking is much like the RAM of your computer - it's volatile. If you don't want to lose it, you need to "save to disc" by writing it down. Take a lesson from Sam and record your dreams immediately, as soon as you wake.

#1. Pause & Notice
Everybody dreams. But you won't remember your dreams if you don't *pay attention* to your dreams when you awaken. You need to give the dream time to emerge. Imagine the ocean is the realm of dreams. That's your subconscious mind. When you first wake, the waves are coming in oh-so-gently to the shore. They come in . . . and then they go out . . . If you pause for just a moment, you may notice the wave carrying your dream across the threshold. That's when you have full recall of a dream. As the wave recedes, you may catch only a few fragments of a dream, as if they were little crabs scurrying back into the sea. That's okay. Just pause long enough to notice what, if anything, is there? Whatever comes, write it down.

The threshold between sleeping and waking a very sleepy, dreamy place. When you wake, you need to give the dream time to emerge. If you don't remember a dream, right away, stay right there in that sleepy-dreamy feeling. Give yourself a few moments to turn your attention inside and notice what, if anything, is being carried across the threshold. Sometimes a dream will emerge. If something comes to mind, no matter how small, make a note of it. Trust that your subconscious mind has brought it to awareness for a reason.

Too many people leap out of bed, right away, and dive into the activities of their day. The problem is that it activates the conscious thinking mind which gets in the way of your ability to remember your dreams. You need to gently pause and notice... Ask yourself, "Where was I just?" Often, you'll get a glimmer of recall. It might be a mere fragment of an image, or a word, a mood, or even a song. It doesn't matter. Realize *that* is the dream and make a note of it.

#2. First impressions

If you want to understand your dreams, you need to avoid the temptation to judge, or analyze, or try to make sense of anything. Dreams aren't logical. Logic is the territory of the conscious mind. As a result, there's always the temptation to try to figure things out. When that happens, realize your conscious mind is trying to butt it. The conscious mind has a tendency to try to step in because it wants to be in control. It wants to figure it all out. But it's too soon for that.

When you're recording your dream, that conscious, thinking, analyzing part of you, needs to take a back seat. Just capture those impressions and write them down exactly as they come to you. What's your first impression when you awaken? What's there? Have you ever woken up feeling grumpy? That could be the whisper of a dream! Trust your first impression because, if you continue to focus on it, you'll get more.

It's a temptation to discount those first impressions. They seldom make sense. But dreams seldom make sense, right away. This is because the subconscious mind uses a different language than the conscious mind. If you notice any of the following, you may have the fragment of a dream. Subconscious signals can be subtle. Don't dismiss it. Write it down.

- Fragment of an image
- Song melody or lyrics
- Sounds
- A thought or words being spoken
- A general mood.
- Emotions or sensations in the body.

At first, a fragment of a dream might seem like nothing. But sometimes, nothing is something. For example, Paul McCartney woke with a melody that wouldn't leave him. It kept playing over and over in his head. This earworm was a hangover from a dream pestering him to write it down. When he finally wrote it down, he put words to the melody and the song, *Yesterday*, was birthed.

This is how the subconscious mind communicates. The act of writing down a mere fragment can have a cascade effect. It might just be a whisper to begin with. But if you pay attention to the whispers, you could discover something important behind it. Through the process of writing, you may be delighted to find a full-fledged movie flooding into your awareness. Writing it down shows your subconscious mind that you can be trusted. As a result, more will be revealed to you. Recording even the most fragmentary residue of a dream builds rapport with your Subconscious Mind. It sends a powerful message that says, "What you have to say matters to me. Tell me more!" You may have to practice this for a week or more but, once the suggestion has been accepted that your dreams are important to you, your subconscious mind will open the floodgates.

#3. Report exactly
Dream recall can fade very quickly in the same way crabs disappear into the surf. And the longer you wait, the more likely your conscious mind will find a way to edit the contents of the dream. The conscious mind is very good at convincing us to put things off. But if you don't write it down immediately, the conscious mind will get in there and change things. Worse, you could lose the dream, completely. Don't put it off until later. Write it down immediately – exactly as you remember it.

Dreams seldom make sense to begin with. It doesn't *have* to make sense, right away. Later it will make sense. For now, you need to catch the dream the way it played out. If the sequence of events in a dream seems to play out in a weird order - for example, the beginning happens after the middle and the middle plays out at the end – it drives the conscious mind bonkers. As a result, it will try to "correct" things, so they make more sense. Don't let it! Dreams are cryptic for a reason. Trust that the order you remember is the correct order. You won't know why it played out that way until you dive into the interpretation process. But to interpret your dream correctly, you first need to write it down exactly as you recall it - without conscious interference. Remember, later it will make sense. It may even surprise you!

#4. Associate
Once you have recorded your dream, or dream fragment, look for any associations. Ask yourself, "What, if anything, does this remind me of?" Don't overthink things. Just pay attention to your first impression. The subconscious mind automatically responds to

questions. What's your first impression? If something comes to mind, great! Write it down. If nothing comes, that's okay, too. Whatever comes, honor it. You're building a bridge into your dream life by giving it your attention.

If you think you what the dream is about, make a note of that association but make no assumptions. Dreams don't tell us what we already know. They show us what we *don't* know or don't want to look at. If you assume you know what it means, you could miss out on an important message.

#5. Persist!

Dream working is a practice that will yield results. You're developing a skill. If you don't remember your dreams right away, persist. It's not that you didn't have a dream. You just need to start *catching* your dreams. When you wake, pause and notice . . . What, if anything, is there? Make a note of your first impressions. Even if you never interpreted a single dream, the simple act of paying attention to your dreams facilitates a greater alignment between your inner and outer lives. When you commit to a practice of waking up and immediately turning your attention inward, you send a powerful message to your subconscious mind that says, "I'm listening." With a little persistence, it won't be long before the subconscious mind opens the floodgates! If you're still having trouble remembering your dreams, look closer at your sleep hygiene. Are you burning the midnight oil, staring at the blue screen? Are you using any substances which are disrupting your sleep cycles such as alcohol or antidepressants? Some sleeping pills cause amnesia. Switching to a natural sleep support like melatonin, 5-HTP and L-Theanine will support your natural biorhythms. You can even improve dream recall by incubating for dreams. That's next.

Summary

You won't remember your dreams if you're over-tired. Take steps to ensure that sure you're getting a **good night's sleep**. Keep a pen and notepad next to the bed so you can catch the dream as soon as you wake. When you wake, don't leap out of bed immediately. Give the dream time to emerge. **Pause and notice**. What, if anything, is there?

Pay attention to your **first impressions** upon waking. It might just be a fragment to begin with, but as you place your attention on it, you may discover there's more to it. Whatever comes, don't dismiss it!

Report your dream **exactly as you recall** it. Dream seldom make sense to begin with and the conscious mind wants to get in there and mess with it. Don't let it! Dream recall can fade very quickly. Don't put off recording your dream until later. Write it down immediately upon waking.

Once you have recorded your dream, look for any **associations**. Ask yourself, "What, if anything, does this remind me of?" Dreams are often triggered by events in waking life. This may provide a clue as to what the dream is about. If you don't remember your dreams right away, **persist!** Whatever you give attention to, you'll get more of! If you want more dreams, give them more of your attention. Recording your dreams sends a powerful message to your subconscious mind that can open the floodgates.

Perhaps the greatest faculty our minds possess is the ability to cope with pain. Classic thinking teaches us of the four doors of the mind, which everyone moves through according to their need.

First is the door of sleep. Sleep offers us a retreat from the world and all its pain. Sleep marks passing time, giving us distance from the things that have hurt us. When a person is wounded, they will often fall unconscious. Similarly, someone who hears traumatic news will often swoon or faint. This is the mind's way of protecting itself from pain by stepping through the first door.

Second is the door of forgetting. Some wounds are too deep to heal, or too deep to heal quickly. In addition, many memories are simply painful, and there is no healing to be done. The saying 'time heals all wounds' is false. Time heals most wounds. The rest are hidden behind this door.

Third is the door of madness. There are times when the mind is dealt such a blow it hides itself in insanity. While this may not seem beneficial, it is. There are times when reality is nothing but pain, and to escape that pain the mind must leave reality behind.

Last is the door of death. The final resort. Nothing can hurt us after we are dead, or so we have been told.

~ Patrick Rothfuss, The Name of the Wind

Dream Incubation

In the series *Star Trek: Next Generation*, the starship Enterprise had a device called the "holodeck." This was an area of the ship where crew members could enter into virtual realities to experience a little R & R, practice or learn new skills such as sparring, and consult with experts, both living and dead through the agency of holograms. In one episode, the character Data consults with some of the greatest minds of history regarding a vexing problem. By conversing with Plato, Steven Hawking and Albert Einstein, Data discovers uniquely different and inspired perspectives to shed light on the issue. Dream incubation is like having your own personal holodeck where you can consult your subconscious mind to gain insight into specific issues, get answers to questions, and find solutions to problems.

Just as the sleep temples of ancient Egypt and Greece used dream incubation as part of the sleep treatment in order to petition the gods to provide a solution through a dream, you can use dream incubation to make a request to your subconscious mind to work on a specific issue while you sleep. For example, I was thinking about creating a new course, but I was conflicted over whether this would be the best use of my time. To gain insight, I incubated on the idea of taking the first step by "creating the introduction." When I woke, I had recall of a fragment of the song, *Rudolf the Red-Nosed Reindeer*. All I could recall was the cascading melody that comes before the song begins. I couldn't even remember what the words were. Puzzling.

At the time I had this dream, it wasn't close to Christmas. Clearly, I wasn't picking up on associations from television programs or Christmas decorations. It just didn't make any sense for me to have this song in my head! So, what did I do? I dismissed the dream, of course!

That's the conscious mind stepping in, saying, "Nonsense! Just a silly dream!" I couldn't have been more wrong. Fortunately, my subconscious mind wouldn't let it go. The song got stuck in my head, pestering me all day long. I kept hearing this annoying, cascading melody over and over again. No words. Just, "DA-da, and DA-da, and DA-da and Blitzen . . ." Arrghhh! Finally, I relented and took action to look up the lyrics to the song. What was it trying to tell me? Immediately, I understood. The beginning of the song is an *introduction* to the song. It was the answer to my dream incubation question. *Yes. Create an introduction to the course.*

Lesson learned. If you wake up with a song, treat it like a dream. If it stays with you throughout the day, there's a good chance your earworm is a message. Treat it as such by writing it down. If you want to gain insight into a particular problem you're dealing with, incubate a dream. If you want to receive guidance to support healing, incubate a dream. If you don't remember your dreams, a great way to improve your dream recall is to incubate for dreams! Dream incubation focuses your attention on your dream life. And what we focus on, we tend to get more of.

How to Incubate

The approach we're going to use follows the same four-step protocol used by the Ancient Egyptians to consult their dreams for the purposes of self-healing:

1. Petition
2. Ritual
3. Report
4. Interpret

Dream incubation is a way to request answers to questions and solutions to problems. If you want good information, you need to take your innermost mind seriously. Treat it with respect. Your dreams can provide a preview of where you're headed. They can show you what you're not looking at or not considering, so you can make better decisions. They can show you your choices. What they won't do is predict the future. Dreams give us access to information that our conscious mind is not normally aware of, can't figure out, or wants to avoid (often because it's emotionally uncomfortable). The content of your dreams comes out of your emotional memory banks. Think of it as a bank account; if you didn't deposit the information into your account, you wouldn't be able to withdraw it.

Step 1. Petition – Ask for a Dream

The first step to dream incubation is to formulate a clear question. Then, write it down in a dedicated notebook or journal. To petition means "to make a formal request." The Ancients petitioned the gods because the gods were a part of daily life and could be called upon for help. Your Higher Power is your concept of a power greater than yourself. Think of it as a part of you that knows everything about you and loves you. It wants what's best for you. It wants you to be healthy, happy, and successful. This part of you, which is aligned with The Highest Good, sees the bigger picture. Some people call this God, Spirit, Higher Self, Holy Spirit, Wise Mind, or Subconscious Mind.

If you want a clear answer, you need to have a clear question in mind. Your question needs to be specific, relevant, and open to outcome. Decide on a *specific* theme or subject for your dream. What single issue, specific action, or result do you want more information about? Avoid multiple-choice questions such as "Which would be the best choice?" and yes-no questions such as "Will I win the election?" Make sure your request is *relevant* to you at this time. You need to have an emotional investment in solving the problem you're working on. What problem are you actively working on? You also need to be open to outcome. This means that you are earnestly seeking the truth rather than trying to manipulate a specific outcome. The best questions are a request for information. This ensures that your request is free of assumptions and you are *open* to learning something new. For example, "What can I do to resolve this problem?" "What information might help me to achieve this goal?" "What blocks are preventing me from achieving this outcome?" "What do I need to know about . . ."

If you're not clear about what the problem is, what you want, where your focus should be, or what the next best step might be, ask! Ask to be shown the real nature of the problem, the most satisfying outcome available, the most fulfilling path or direction, or what options are available to you at this time.

If you have a BIG ASK -- such as a pressing issue, a big worry or concern, or an issue that has a big emotional charge around it -- chunk down. Don't try to eat an elephant all at once. Pick one aspect of the issue to explore. Remember, you have unlimited dream credits!

Examples of appropriate questions for dream incubation:

- What do I need to know about (situation/condition)?
- What action do I need to take to (be successful, achieve a desired outcome, heal, or overcome a problem)?
- What would be the result of (making this choice)?
- What would be the consequence of (taking this action)?
- What is the nature of (specific situation)?

Dream incubation isn't just for problem-solving. You can make a request to have an experience. Would you like to travel to Greece? Incubate on it! Want to visit a past life? Outer space? Your subconscious mind can be a wonderful travel agent!

Getting Started

Ask to have a dream which you remember. Clearly state your desire to wake up with a dream. Your request should include that you will sleep deeply, and wake feeling refreshed *with a dream* which you will write down immediately.

Step 2. Ritual – Saturate the Mind with Expectancy

Once you have decided what you'd like to dream about, the next step is to saturate your mind with that specific, singular idea. Picture a bathroom sink that has a plunger-type stopper. When the plunger is down, the sink is closed, and you can fill the basin with water. When the plunger is pulled up, the water flows down the drain. The bathroom sink is like your conscious mind. Before you sleep, you want to fill up the basin with your request. Then, as you fall asleep, the plunger will open, allowing your request to flow down into the subconscious level of your mind. While you sleep, your subconscious mind will work on it.

Fill the basin with your request using the language of your subconscious mind. Picture it and feel it. Impress upon your innermost mind the importance of this issue. Saturate the mind with the expectancy that you will receive an answer. One of the easiest ways to do this is to simply write about the issue at bedtime. You can make a list, or just pour your thoughts and feelings about that issue onto the page.

Whatever you want to dream about, the key is focused intent. You need to set a clear intention, then focus all of your conscious attention on that singular purpose. Saturate the conscious mind with your desire to have a dream about that specific issue. As you fall asleep, your desire to have a dream will be carried across the threshold into the subconscious level of your mind.

Focus your conscious mind on that one thing you want to dream about. As you think about this, you are creating pictures in your mind. That's using the language of the subconscious mind. If you can generate a feeling to go with those pictures, you'll be communicating directly with your subconscious mind. The more important the issue is to you, the more emotionally invested you will be in receiving an answer. This will make a strong impression on that part of you that generates dreams.

If you're working on a problem, write down all the details and facts related to the problem. Saturate your conscious mind with a single idea along with all the feelings associated with that issue. Once you have saturated your conscious mind with your intention to dream, and filled it with all the details and emotions, turn off the light and keep your focus on that single theme until you fall asleep. *Expect to wake with a dream*. As you fall asleep, the stopper in the basin will pop up, and like water in the bathroom sink, your request will flow across the threshold, down into the subconscious mind, where it can be worked on.

Step 3. Report – Catch the Dream

When you wake in the morning -- pause. What, if anything, is there? Dreams come in all shapes and sizes. Sometimes, you'll wake up with a full-length movie. Other times, you'll have a thirty-second commercial. You might just have a fragment, a song, or even a phrase. Catch the dream!

A feeling upon waking can be the doorway back into the dream. Whatever comes to mind, that's the dream. Write it down immediately. You can work on the interpretation process later if you're pressed for time, but you must-must-must write it down immediately. Your bedside notepad is for rough notes. Later, you will record your dream in greater detail in your dream journal. For now, capture the key words in the order they occur. Lists are great for identifying the key elements of the dream and act as reminders when you sit down to record your dream in detail.

Whatever comes, make a note of it. Even if it's just a whisper of an image, that's the dream! Write it down exactly as you recall it. Did you know that Paul McCartney woke from a troubling dream in which his beloved mother said to him, "Let it be"? Solid gold.

Step 4. Interpret – Find the Hidden Meaning

In the sleep temples, the patient's dream provided the basis for prescription. Dreams can provide information and guidance, but they need to be translated to be understood. The first step to interpreting your dreams is to record them in detail. It's best to record your dream as soon as you get up while it's still fresh. If you put it off until later, the conscious mind will most likely mess with your recall.

Dreams are sent in the service of healing and wholeness, but they are seldom literal. They also don't tell us what we already know. Even if you're confident you know what your dream is telling you, there could be a deeper layer you are completely unaware of. Remember to write it down exactly as you recall it.

Summary

Be prepared to catch your dreams by setting a notepad and pencil next to your bed. If there's something specific that you'd like to dream about, incubate on it.

To petition a dream, you must set a clear intention to have a dream. Use a ritual to saturate your mind with a singular intention. Write it down using the language of your subconscious mind. As you fall asleep, stay focused on your request to have a dream. Expect to have a dream!

When you wake in the morning, catch the dream. Immediately make a note of your first impressions in your bedside notepad. Rough notes, bullet points, and lists are fine. No matter how insignificant it may seem, write it down.

Dreams don't tell us what we already know. Record your dream exactly as you recall it. Later you will record your dream in more detail. Remember, if you want to correctly interpret your dreams, keep your conscious, thinking mind out of the process.

Dream Journaling

Create a habit of writing in your journal every morning. Even if you don't wake up with a dream, you can still take a few minutes to write in your journal each morning. You can use it to reflect upon the daily situation, mull over your plans or wishes, and if you have too much on your mind, you can do a brain dump. Chances are good that, as you clear some of the mind clutter, a dream will fall onto the page. If you're prone to analysis paralysis, brain dumping is the remedy. It doesn't take very long and can be very therapeutic. All that's required is that you produce three pages of stream-of-consciousness writing.

Ideally, brain dumping is a morning routine. Write longhand -- as quickly as you can. Let it be messy. The idea is to get whatever is on your mind onto the page without conscious interference. This isn't an exercise in creative writing. No one is going to grade you on your handwriting. Whatever comes into your head, write it down -- without editing. As soon as you think "that" thought, put it on the page. Sometimes what will pour out onto the page will be completely mundane. For example, *This is stupid. I haven't got time for this, the dog needs to go out, I didn't pay the electric bill . . . blah, blah, blah.*

You'd be surprised at how therapeutic this can be! The more you dump onto the page, the less you're going to have to carry around inside. You're giving it a place to go so you won't have to carry it into your day. You'll also be surprised at how much better you will feel! All that's required is that you write down everything that's on your mind. Don't think. Write! Don't be nice. Be honest. Use whatever language comes to mind. Your journal is no place for political correctness. It's a place for truth-telling. If the thought happens to be "gawd damn it!" then, for gawd-sake, don't write, "gosh darn it!" That's not being authentic. That's editing. Instead, think of the page as a toilet. You're giving all that mind-chatter a place to go. Whatever comes into your head goes onto the page. What you may discover is that, as you clear the mental clog in your drain, a dream will bubble up to the surface of awareness. When that happens, you'll know what to do.[5]

How to Record Your Dreams

LongHand

Write your dreams out longhand. You may be tempted to text them into your phone or type them into your computer. But that's using the wrong side of the brain. Texting and typing are left-brain activities. It may seem easier, but it involves too much conscious mind activity. That invites editing, and as soon as you start editing, you'll lose the dream. If you want to understand what your dreams are telling, you need to keep the conscious mind out of the picture while you're recording your dream.

Start with rough hand-written notes upon waking. It only takes a few minutes. Bullet points are enough to remind you of the flow of the dream narrative. Then, as soon as possible, record your dream longhand in your journal. Once you've captured the dream and recorded it in your dream journal, you're ready to begin the

---

[5] Learn more in *The Artist's Way: A Spiritual Path to Higher Creativity* by Julia Cameron.

interpretation process. If you prefer to keep a journal of your dreams on the computer, that's fine. But initially, you need to record the dream by hand. Then, you can type it into a file if you want to.

Double Space

When you begin dream journaling, double space to give yourself room to make notes during the interpretation process. This can help save time when you begin interpreting your dream, especially when you use the Dream Walk. Once you're comfortable with the process, you'll find the approach that works best for you.

When you're working on a dream, let it be messy. The conscious mind wants order and logic, but the subconscious mind is just fine with being all over the place. Feel free to draw pictures and make notes in the margins. Use circles and arrows. Highlight keywords that pop out at you. Make lists. Anything goes.

Present Tense

When you record your dreams, always use present-tense language. "I am . . ." "He says . . ." "She goes . . ." Present-tense language is a way of stepping back into the dream. It's all happening NOW. For example, let's say that in the dream you're driving in your car. The way to record it would be to write, "I am driving in my car." If you write, "I was driving in my car," it causes you to dissociate from the image. It's back "then" rather than "here and now." You want to be able to re-enter the dream. The way to do that is to use present-tense language.

Present-tense language will help you to stay present to the dream. That's what we want to do. This is the language of the subconscious mind. The subconscious is timeless. It doesn't have a concept of the past or future. It's all now-now-now. Time is the territory of the conscious mind. When you use past tense, you put the dream image into the past. This can create a block by distancing you from the dream narrative. We want to honor the dream. Staying present to the dream helps you to associate deeper into the dream content, which will make more detail available to you.

Feelings & Emotions

Once you have recorded your dream using present-tense language, the next step is to capture the feeling. The most important element of the dream is the feelings it holds. Feelings are how the subconscious mind communicates. It speaks the language of emotion through pictures and sensations in the body. The dream narrative is a container for feelings that point to the meaning of the dream. Every image has a feeling associated with it. Make a note of the general feeling or mood that you were in when you woke. Keep your focus on the feeling as you record the dream in your dream journal. What emotions are being communicated? Sad? Mad? Glad? Scared? Something else? Write it down! Capture how it feels.

72-Hour Clause

When you have finished recording your dream, make a note of the date at the top of the page. Then, make a few notes about anything significant that might have happened during the last 24 to 72 hours. Dreams are always relevant to what's happening in your waking life. Ask yourself -- What have I been thinking about? What have I been worried about? What significant situation or circumstances have arisen in the past couple of days?

Because the subconscious mind works through association, dreams can get triggered by situations in our daily life. That's how we learn. It's how memories are formed. Ask yourself: What, if anything, does this remind me of? This is likely what your subconscious mind is sorting through, so think back over the last 24 to 72 hours. Make a note of any obvious associations or significant events that may be showing up in your dream life.

Working Title

Giving your dream a working title can be helpful because you may want to go back to it later. This will make it much easier for you to find in your journal. The working title reveals the general theme of the dream. For example, the dream I had that came as a Christmas song was given the working title of *Rudolf Song Course Intro*.

Dreams often repeat a single theme over a series of days or even weeks. Your working title can reflect this while helping to jog your memory if you want to compare it to other dreams. If you notice a recurring theme or cast of characters, pay attention! Repetitive and recurring dreams happen because they're trying to get your attention. Something is unresolved.

Dreams can play out like episodes in a series. You might have a series of dreams that play out like *The Walking Dead*. The main characters are the same, they're always facing the same danger, but over time, they become more resourceful. They grow, evolve, and learn how to deal with the problems in their environment more effectively. For example, if *The Walking Dead* were *my* dream, I would interpret that to mean that I can't change my environment, but I can change my response. I can be more alert to the dangers and my responses can be more proactive.

Sometimes you'll get a series of dreams that are more theme-based. For example, *The Twilight Zone*, where every episode is a different story involving assorted characters, but there's always an underlying mystery being revealed-- with a twist. If *The Twilight Zone* were my dream, I would interpret that to mean that situations in my waking life are showing me something that's not obvious. It might be something more of a spiritual nature that I'm unaware of. Coming up with a working title gives you a way to capture the general theme of the dream based on your first impressions. Think of it as a "headline."

Creating a headline makes your dreams searchable. I have been recording my dreams for over 35 years. As a result, my attic is full of boxes filled with dream journals. Sometimes, I'll have a dream that reminds me of an earlier dream I had. I've had dreams that repeat an earlier dream or refer back to an earlier dream -- kind of like "dream short-hand." When that happens, I go into the attic and pull out the old dream journal. Headlining my dreams helps me to locate the dream easily. If you buy a calendar at the dollar store, you can make a notation of the dream title by date. Notate a few keywords and you'll be able to see at a glance what the dream was about. Then, file your dream journals in order of date. That way, you'll have no problem going back to find an old dream. Optionally, you could create a file on your computer in which to keep a list of your headlines by date.

Details, Details, Details

When you're recording your dream, flesh out all the details. Skipping over something is like missing part of the movie or skipping a chapter in a book. Don't rush the process. Note everything you can recall. For example, what time of the day is it? What season? Are you male or female in the dream? How old do you feel? Are you alone or with others? Where do you find yourself in the dream? What's the setting?

What colors do you become aware of? What feelings are you experiencing as the story unfolds? What objects or characters are central to the dream? Are some characters or objects peripheral?

Nothing in a dream is insignificant. Peripheral characters and objects may seem unimportant, but everything in the dream has meaning. The tendency of the conscious mind is to minimize, but, as you will discover, the secret is in the details. Use a spoon. You'll want to get every bite. If you're driving down the road, what vehicle are you in? What color is it? Is it new or familiar? What are you seeing? Hearing? Tasting? Touching? Feeling? Are you alone or with someone? Who are you with? What kind of road are you driving on? Is this a new road or a familiar one to you? Are you a passenger or the driver of the car? What are you doing? How does it feel to be doing that?

The answer to these questions reveals the meaning hidden in the dream story. There's no need to figure anything out. Just keep your focus on the dream and all will be revealed through the dream interpretation process. If the dream reminds you of something, make a note of it, but stay with the flow of the dream narrative.

Don't let yourself get sidetracked by following associations. Remember, the contents of the dream are unique to you. They're coming out of your life experiences. These are your symbols. They hold all the meaning you have given them. The objects and characters in the dream belong to you. There's a reason the dream put you on a country lane instead of a four-lane highway. There's a reason why you're in the driver's seat, passenger seat, or back seat. There's a reason the time of year is fall or winter instead of spring or summer.

Capture all the details. That's where you'll find the answers you seek. Especially capture any *feelings*. As you move through the dream scenes, different feelings can arise. How do you feel? e.g., scared, alone, angry, sad, guilty, tired, etc. Pay attention to *exaggerations*. Dreams are sometimes bizarre in order to get your attention. Amplification is the dream shouting and waving to get your attention.

Summary

1. Create a morning habit of spending time with your journal.
2. Record the dream longhand, exactly as it comes.
3. Double space.
4. Record your dream in the present tense.
5. Note the feelings and emotions present in the dream.
6. Think back over the past 24 – 72 hours.
7. Give your dream a working title. Give it a headline!
8. Flesh out as many details as you can -- especially feelings!

The ABCs of Dream Healing

Imagine that you're standing in front of the door to your bedroom closet. When you open the door, you discover an enormous walk-in closet! As you step inside and look around, you realize this closet is enormous! Hanging inside this closet are what appear to be garments. It looks like you have a lot of clothes hanging in your closet. Only they're not clothes. Actually, they look more like people. These are all the people in your life, both known and unknown, living and dead. Some of them are familiar to you. Some of them might appear to be strangers. But everyone in your life, both known and unknown, living or dead, is here in your closets. This is your closet. In it, you discover friends, family, acquaintances, and even total strangers. They're all here. But they're not really people. They're inanimate. In fact, they look rather like costumes.

These are the many Parts you play in life. They're like roles. You take them on when you need them. And when you put one on, you *become* that Part of you. You step into the role of that Part. Notice how different each of your Parts appears to be. Each embodies certain characteristics. Some of your Parts may seem quite simple, while others are more complex. Each expresses specific qualities that are unique to that Part of you. Some of your Parts will be assigned a specific function or a feeling. Some will express a statement you wish to make, while others will embody a particular attitude or a stance you take on whenever you're faced with a particular situation. Together, they represent the many faces you present to the world. All your opinions, feelings, judgments, desires, and responses in life are here in your closet as your many Parts. And they're all based on your experiences in life from the earliest age.

Take a moment to notice how they make you feel. Notice how these Parts of you have the power to affect how you feel about yourself. Some of your Parts will make you feel good, happy. These are comfortable roles you take on that put a smile on your face. Some of your Parts make you feel not-so-good. They make you feel uncomfortable, grumpy, frustrated, scared, angry, and even worthless. Some of them are downright painful! For example, you might notice there's a Judge in there. The Critic. The Playful Child. The rebellious teenager. The Warrior Part. The Fun-loving Part. And many other Parts of you. Notice which ones you recognize. Which ones are your favorites?

Now imagine that you're taking one out. Try it on for size. Notice how easily you can slip into the role of "other" as if you were putting on a piece of clothing. And just like the clothes you wear on your body these roles have the power to affect how you feel about yourself. Some make you feel good, happy. They're comfortable parts. Some are neutral. And some make you feel not-so-good, scared, angry, sad, or worse, worthless.

See yourself in the mirror. Imagine it, sense it, feel it, whatever works for you. Realize that this person in the mirror is not you. Not really. It's just a Part of you. And you have many, many Parts. You have happy Parts and sad Parts, smart Parts, funny Parts, talented Parts, creative Parts, and many more Parts. They're all here in your closet.

Together they make up the totality of your personality. It's all based on your experiences growing up[6].

Now, it's been said that we are the sum total of our life experiences. It's true that your past experiences have given you knowledge and a unique lens through which you view the world of people and things around you. But you are so much more than the sum of your Parts. *You are you.* You see what you see, you hear what you hear, you feel what you feel, and you know what you know. You are the one who *puts on* the role of a Part. You *become* the Part by putting your energy into that role. But it's not you. You are a unique individual, a worthy soul on an important journey. And all these Parts of you here in your closet? They belong to you.

What's in Your Closet?

Fritz Perls, the father of Gestalt Therapy, said that everything in our dream is a projection of ourselves. The dream reveals Parts of us. When all Parts are working together harmoniously, we feel good, aligned, in the flow, creative and alive. When parts of us are conflicted, we feel out of sorts. Everyone and everything in your dream is a Part of you. Every part serves a positive purpose. That means every Part is good. Even the uncomfortable ones.

Everything that shows up in a dream, whether it's a day dream, a night dream, or this dream, is coming out of the contents of your own mind. It's your dream. Every aspect of the dream is about you. Whether it's other people, an animal, or an inanimate object, every part of the dream is a Part of you. It's there for a reason.

---

[6] Adapted from a script by Mary Lee LaBay

Your dreams are about you. They're about your thoughts, feelings, and perceptions. They're being communicated to you through the universal language of your subconscious mind --symbol.

A = "All That I See"

A young couple is sitting and eating breakfast. The wife notices the neighbor hanging the wash outside and comments that her laundry is not very clean. "She doesn't know how to wash properly. Maybe she needs better laundry soap!" complains the wife. Her husband looks on but remains silent. Every time the neighbor hangs out her wash, the wife makes the same comments. Then, one day the woman is surprised to see a nice clean wash on the neighbor's line. She says to her husband, "Looks like she finally learned how to wash properly! I wonder what happened!" Her husband replies, "I got up early this morning and cleaned our windows."

In the ABCs of Dream Healing, A stands for "All that I see . . . is me." What I'm seeing are my perceptions. Dream Healing is about cleaning the windows of our perception. To do this, you must first own the Parts of the dream. Whether it's a night dream, day dream, or this dream, it's *your* dream. Taking responsibility for every Part of the dream allows you to transform the dream and, through it, yourself. Your dreams reflect back to you what's going on inside you -- in your mind. That's useful information.

Dreams reflect back to us daily issues. Whatever issues you're wrestling with in daily life are being reflected back to you, including your hopes and wishes, internal conflicts, fears, inadequacies, and unfulfilled desires. Your dreams will show you where you're getting blocked and, more importantly, why you're getting blocked.

It's all based on our beliefs. What we see depends on the window through which we look, through our lens of perception. This lens is also known as the Critical Faculty of the Mind. It's a semi-permeable barrier that sits between the conscious and subconscious minds and forms a lens through which we see the world. Each of us learned to view life in a personal way based on our experiences of life growing up. Those experiences formed our belief system.

All that we *can* see is what the Critical Faculty allows us to see. It's the lens through which we see everything. What the lens allows you to see is coming out of your past experiences. Our experiences in daily life then reflect back to us our beliefs. The problem is that 90% of the beliefs that make up our Critical Faculty were formed before the age of five. Much of what we believe as adults is based on the perceptions of a child. Our beliefs decide who we are, what to expect, what we deserve in life, what's acceptable, what's true and not true, who we have to be to get our needs met, and much, much more. This is the stuff that dreams are made of.

Perception is projection. ~**Matt James**

Dreams are not idle entertainment. Your dreams are showing you what needs to change so you can live a more fulfilling life. If you want a better tomorrow, it begins with changing your lens on life today. Dreams reflect issues that we're dealing with in daily life. They show us what the subconscious mind is working on. Often, it's stuff the conscious mind didn't have time to deal with. This is because the conscious mind is limited. It has been estimated that the conscious mind can only process about five to seven bits of information at any given moment. The subconscious, on the other hand, is virtually unlimited. All the stuff the conscious mind didn't deal with gets downloaded to be worked on later, and it shows up in our dreams.

Daily events can act as triggers for unresolved issues. Our dreams then reflect back to us whatever issues we are wrestling with in daily life. For example, internal conflicts, blocks to performance, fears and inadequacies, unfulfilled desires, identity issues, and search for purpose.

Summary

The A in the ABCs of Dream Healing stands for "All that I see." All that I see is me. Your dreams are all about you and your perceptions. Every Part of the dream is a Part of you. They are being communicated to the conscious mind using the symbolic language of the subconscious mind -- image and emotion.

"All that I see ..." are *my* perceptions. Dream Healing is a process of transforming our perceptions. The first step is to take ownership of the contents of your dreams by recognizing that every aspect of the dream, including people and objects, is a part of you. Taking ownership for every Part of the dream allows you to transform the dream and, through it, yourself.

Your dreams reflect what's going on inside *you* -- in your *mind*. As a result, no one can interpret your dreams for you. The only person who is qualified to interpret your dreams is YOU!

The Dream Walk

What makes dream interpretation challenging for many people is that the subconscious mind doesn't speak the same language as the conscious mind. It's like the subconscious mind is speaking Greek and the conscious mind only understands English. To understand a dream, you need to translate it into a language that the conscious mind can understand. The Dream Walk[7] gives you a very step-by-step way to translate a dream from the symbolic language of the subconscious mind into information that the conscious mind can understand and act on.

Dream Walking is the first dream interpretation technique I learned that actually works. This is what got me hooked, back in 1988, and I've been working with my dreams ever since! The Dream Walk allows you to quickly and easily translate a dream from subconscious "Greek" to conscious "English." It gives you the broad strokes of the Story while allowing you to identify the Parts that are active in a specific issue. If you're a hypnosis practitioner, this deceptively simple technique helped me tremendously in my work as a regression hypnotherapist.

Getting Started

Take a moment to think of either a favorite fairy tale from childhood or a favorite movie. Then, pick a scene from that movie. Now, let that scene play out in your mind's eye. Where are you in that scene? Are

---

[7] Phil Winkelman

you watching from the sidelines or as a central character? Is it daytime or nighttime? Are you inside or outside? Are you alone or with someone? As the scene plays out, you see what you see, you hear what you hear, you know what you know, and you feel what you feel. Give yourself a moment to notice what's happening.

You now have a dream to work with! Write it down exactly as you remember it. Remember, double space and use the present tense. It's all happening now!

Step 1: Identify Character, Object, Action

The first step to Dream Walking is to identify the keywords. A keyword is either a character, object, or action. The way to do this is to go through your dream and either circle or highlight every word that identifies either a Character, Object, or Action. A character could be a person such as "Mom" or "Uncle Bob." It could be an entity such as an alien or an angel. They could be living or dead. They may be known to you or a complete stranger. They could even be a character from a movie. An object is a thing such as a car, flower, or book. An action word would be something that's happening in the dream. It might be something you are doing, such as walking, driving, singing, or something happening in the dream that you're noticing or observing, such as flying, thinking, shouting, fighting, etc.

Go back through your dream and circle every word for:

1) Character
2) Object
3) Action

Step 2: Quality, Function, Feeling

Once you have identified every character, object, and action word, all you need to do is come up with another way of saying that. The tendency is to try to describe the object or the character. That's not what we want. Find *another way of saying that* by coming up with three words to describe that character or object as either a *quality*, a *function*, or a *feeling*. What quality, function, or feeling do you associate with that person or thing? For example, let's say Uncle Bob shows up in your dream. Bob's a character. What are three words that you would use to describe Uncle Bob? What qualities best describe Uncle Bob?

What function or feeling do you associate with Uncle Bob? Come up with three words. For example, you might describe Uncle Bob as smart, creative, and capable. Or you might say he's trustworthy, generous, and kind. Maybe you'd call him a complete jerk, a pain-in-the-patoot, and annoying! Whatever you come up with, these are the qualities that you associate with Uncle Bob. That's what we're after! What you *wouldn't* say is that he's tall, has a beard, and tells randy jokes. This doesn't tell you anything that you don't already know. You want to come up with either a quality, function, or feeling word.

Object

Let's say you have a lampshade in your dream. That's an object. What are three words or phrases that you would use to describe a lampshade? For example, you could say that a lampshade is "inhibiting the light," "directing the light toward something," or even that it's "fashionable." That's a quality. What you *wouldn't* say is that it's metal, glass, or fabric because this doesn't reveal much about what "lampshade" means to you.

You could however, grind down a bit deeper by coming up with three words to describe metal, fabric, or glass if that's something that seems to stand out in the dream. Remember, everything in the dream holds meaning! This is a way to milk more of the details out of the dream. What color is that lampshade? Find three words to describe that. To begin, stay with the main character, object, or action words. Then, if you want more information, you can always dig deeper to explore the specifics. This will give you more of the details.

How would you describe a fire truck as a quality, function, or feeling? For example, you might say that it's fast, responsive, and powerful. These are qualities. You might say that it puts out fires, helps people, and responds in an emergency. These are functions. You might describe it as hurrying, important, or excited. These are feelings. Any combination of words is acceptable. The objective is to find *another way of saying that* without describing it in literal terms.

Character
How would you describe a hamster? My words are warm and fuzzy, curious, quiet, shy, soft, gentle, social, and cuddly. If you don't like hamsters, your words will be very different than might, won't they? For example, a central character in one of my dreams was a young woman with tattoos all over her body. When I thought about how else I could describe a woman with tattoos, the three words I came up with were artistic, unconventional, and free-spirited. You might have come up with something entirely different, but this is *my* dream. These are *my* associations.

My dream holds all the meaning that I have given it. Your dream will mean something entirely different. This is the key to revealing the meaning of any dream. It's to uncover the meaning that it holds for THE DREAMER because that character or object that's appearing in the dream is coming out of their Mind. It's a symbol that is unique to them and holds whatever meaning their subconscious has assigned it. The mistake lies in being too literal or factual. Trying to apply the language of the conscious mind to subconscious communication won't work. This is why describing a Tattooed Lady as "a person with drawings all over her body" doesn't tell me anything that I don't already know. It's not meaningful. What you will discover is that when you come up with another way of saying that, something new will be revealed.

Action

Find three words to describe every action. Action words are "doing words" like walking, talking, fighting, working, and driving. Just as you did with objects and character, come up with another way of saying "that." What's another way of saying "walking"? Driving? "Climbing?" Smiling? Often, the answer lies in *how* you are taking that action. How are you walking? Are you marching, strolling, hurrying, or something else? What feeling might be associated with that kind of action? For example, walking could represent moving either toward or away from something or someone (as designated by the dream). It's different than driving because walking involves taking steps (taking action) and moving forward on your own two feet (self-reliance).

Are you walking on level ground? That might suggest "easy-going." Are you walking uphill? That might suggest some kind of challenge or something requiring effort. If your walking is hindered in some way, focus more on the feeling of being hindered. For example, feeling like I need support, or lacking confidence, or pushing myself. It all depends on how that symbol is being presented in the dream narrative. I might describe "driving" as a way of getting where I want to get in life. I might describe it as a means of achieving a goal. If I'm in the driver's seat, I might say that I'm in control of or directing the process. This approach begins to reveal what's happening in the dream in terms that relate to my waking life. Maybe the dream is telling me that I'm driving myself too hard. Having the pedal to the metal may be showing me that I'm pushing too hard to achieve a goal. Maybe I'm on cruise control and need to put more effort into getting where I want to be.

See what I mean? The information that can be milked from the dream is significant. It's all about where you're at in your life. Let's say you're driving in a boat. That's not the same as driving a car, is it? The fact that you're in a boat and not a car is significant. How are these two approaches different? The dream might be showing you how you're going about getting somewhere. It might have to do with your approach to achieving a goal or your attitude toward it. If you're the captain of the boat, it tells you more. It might suggest something about being in charge of a process you're engaged in. For me, there's a difference between a sailboat and a motorboat. Sailing is about taking your time, enjoying the journey, and making incremental adjustments along the way. Sometimes, it can seem like you're headed completely in the wrong direction, but it's necessary because you're working with the wind and the current. A motorboat, on the other hand, is about power and drive. It's a much more direct approach to getting there.

Play Dumb

The biggest challenge in the Dream Walk is playing dumb. Remember, dreams don't tell us what we already know. They show us what we don't know, can't fix, or have been trying to avoid. Resist the temptation to try to figure anything out. Just stay naive and let the dream reveal its own meaning to you. For example, what if you were from another planet and you had no idea what that action or behavior might be? It's completely foreign to you. How would you describe that character, object, or action with words that would help me to understand? When I'm helping someone interpret a dream, I often say, "I'm from Mars. On Mars, we're gelatinous creatures that hang around the drain. I have no idea what "that" is."

Pretend that you have no clue what driving is, or what fighting is, or what writing is. How would you describe that activity? For example, if the action happened to be "talking," I would say, "What's talking? On my planet, we don't talk." How would you describe "talking" to me? Come up with three ways to do that. What if you had to describe "singing" to a person who had never experienced, or seen, or heard, or felt what it's like to sing? How you describe it to them? How would you describe "eating" to them? Or "snoring"? Or "laughing"? How would you explain the concept of "driving" to a gelatinous creature that hangs around the drain? Interesting challenge, isn't it?

If you want to successfully interpret your dreams, stay with the content of the dream itself. The good news is that you don't have to figure anything out. Just play dumb. Pretend you don't know. Come up with a few alternative ways of saying that. Pay close attention to your felt sense of those words and phrases. Your subconscious mind will let you know when it's right.

> *Pro Tip!* Use a Thesaurus to look up synonyms. A synonym is "another way of saying that." The way to use a thesaurus is to pay attention to your felt sense. As you read the alternate word, notice how it feels. Does it feel true? Does it seem to fit? If it does, that's your word. It's your association to a quality, function, or feeling!

Context

The meaning is always relative to the dreamer and the context in which it appears in the dream. Symbols can hold multiple meanings because the mind works through association. To decipher the meaning of a symbol, you need to consider the context in which that character, object, or action appears. This is the main reason dream dictionaries aren't very helpful. They can be useful if you're looking for confirmation once you have done the work of interpreting your dream. They're also useful for looking up the meaning of archetypal symbols. For example, the sun, moon, stars, angels, mother, and father are archetypal symbols; they mean the same thing to most people. Even then, you must consider the personal associations they may hold for you. For example, consider coffee. What are three words to describe coffee using a quality, a function, or a feeling?

Think about this for a moment . . . How would you describe coffee without calling it a beverage? Or black? Or hot? The quality I associate with coffee is stimulating. I associate coffee with having a stimulating conversation with someone. For me, coffee has a stimulating *quality*. I also associate a function with coffee. Coffee wakes me up. For me, the *function* of coffee is waking me up. I also associate a feeling with coffee -- enjoyment. I like coffee. I like to have stimulated conversations with friends. As a result, I also associate coffee with a *feeling* of enjoyment and pleasure. As you can see, not every character or object will have a quality, a function, *and* a feeling associated with it. That's fine. All you need to do is come up with another way of saying that -- three times. Once you get the hang of it, you'll likely come up with *more* words or phrases. The goal is to create a "menu" of alternative words or phrases that are associated with each of your symbols.

You're now ready for the fun part -- translating the language of your dream from Greek to English. If you have double-spaced while recording your dream, you'll have plenty of room to write your words above each of the highlighted or circled words for character, object, and action. The next step is to simply transcribe the story from "French" to English using the Dream Walk.

Step 3: Dream Walk

When I write my dream down, I use a pen, then use a pencil to jot down my three words. Start at the beginning of the dream and walk through the story by replacing the word for each character and object with "the Part of me that is," followed by your three words. Then replace your action words with three words. That's it! You can now translate your dream by either reading it out loud or rewriting it in your journal. While it's more time-consuming, I prefer to rewrite the whole story using my three words. For example, the following is a dream I had after attending a hypnotherapy bootcamp.

Dream Title: "Lenore's Asylum"

I am at a party. It's night time and there are two guys here. I'm not sure who they are, but they feel familiar. I'm having fun, laughing.

Now it's time to leave. I have to drive Lenore home. It's winter outside. Even though there is deep snow everywhere, the roads are clear. We arrive at a private school that looks like an old asylum. We go inside and there is no one there. It feels empty. The power is out, so I offer to take Lenore to my place. She declines.

The Final Scene is of Lenore's room. It has the look and feel of a cocoon. There is a candle burning. It feels cozy.

Notice how I don't always come up with three words. This is because, sometimes, it's obvious what the meaning is. In this case, I just use the word that seems to fit best. The key, as you process your dream, is to pay attention to any associations or feelings that might come to mind. Don't follow the association. If something comes up, make a note of it, and continue with the Dream Walk.

The Interpretation Process
I am at a party Part of me that is social gathering/celebrating/having fun with friends. (I make an immediate association with the residential course I just attended. I continue with the next line.)

It's night time the Part of me that is dark /hard to see /late in the day. (Aha! There's a play on words here! My symbolic language is saying, "It is a bit late in the day." I'm concerned about my age. This also implies impatience or regret.)

There are two guys masculine, dynamic, assertive Parts of me *here. I'm not sure who they are, but they feel familiar.* (All elements of a dream are important, but this one doesn't seem to have as much detail. I do notice an immediate association, however, to the two teachers at the course. These would be the Parts of me that are teachers, healers, skilled.)

I'm having fun, laughing feeling happy, positive, good. (The course was a blast! I loved it!)

Now it's time to leave move on from, abandon the Part of me that is social gathering/celebrating/having (Fun-time is over. This seems to mark the departure from the residential course. It's also the beginning of the second part of the dream.)

I have to (have a need to, am required to, must) *drive* (take charge, take responsibility, motivate) *Lenore* (the Part of me that is needy, lonely, afraid *home* to the Part of me that feels safe, secure, comfortable. (The dream seems to indicate a need to take responsibility for this needy, insecure Part of myself and motivate her to change by becoming more secure and comfortable. i.e., at home with myself.)

Its ~~winter~~ a Part of me that is in a season of life that feels unfriendly, unloving, and uncomfortable, *and there is ~~deep snow everywhere~~* a Part of me that has a pervasive and deep feeling of bitterness/harshness/discomfort. (This confirms my "late in the day" interpretation. I'm entering into the winter of my life and am feeling depressed. What have I accomplished? What's the point? It's a dark time.)

The ~~roads~~ Part of me that is a path, direction in life, route is ~~clear~~ free of blocks, unobstructed, and navigable. (Despite my past regrets and negative outlook toward the future, the way forward is unobstructed, and nothing is preventing me from moving forward on my path in life.)

~~We~~ The Part of me that is in charge, and the Part of me that is needy, *~~arrive~~* show up, appear, and attain *at a ~~private school~~* a teaching and learning Part of me that is "old school" and has rigid or solid structures.

It looks like an ~~asylum~~ old Part of me that was once a place of sanctuary, retreat, and mental healing.

We go ~~inside~~ within, enter the Part of me that looks like teaching and learning; and was once a place of sanctuary, retreat, and mental healing *~~and there is no one there~~*. This Part of me has been abandoned! *Feels ~~empty~~* sad, alone, hopeless. (When I go within, I discover an empty feeling. This is because I have abandoned the Part of me that <u>serves the purpose of teaching and healing</u>.)

The ~~power is out~~ feeling powerless, with no light, no warmth, *so I offer to take ~~Lenore~~* the Part of me that is lonely, insecure, and needy *to ~~my place~~* my comfort zone, a place of security and comfort. (The Part of me that used to be about teaching and healing feels powerless. I have lost my vision. I decide to bring the Part of me that feels needy, lonely, and insecure to conscious awareness. Note: the dream does not show me what "my place" is.)

Lenore declines. (Uh-oh. The needy, lonely, insecure Part of me rejects/refuses/says no to my solution to leave this old place of sanctuary, retreat, and mental healing that used to serve the purpose of teaching and healing. This Part of me does not agree to be brought to consciousness!)

Final scene: Lenore's room feels like a cocoon. (This was a snapshot that I interpreted as "insight." The place where the Part of me that feels needy, lonely, and insecure lives actually feels like the Part of me that is protected. This is a safe, comfortable place for growth, change, and transformation to occur.)

It has a ~~candle~~ Part of me that is illuminating/bringing light to darkness ~~burning~~ alive/awake/radiant/wanting. *Feels cozy.* (The candle feels like a spiritual symbol. The Part of me that feels lonely finds safety and comfort in this place of growth and transformation. Within it is the Part of me that gently brings light to darkness (awakens), shines softly, and is warm and friendly. Feels comfortable. (Association: *Years ago, I did a course in Life Purpose. My life purpose statement was to teach dreams and healing. What I did not realize at that time was how intertwined this was with hypnotherapy! This only became clear to me after the residential course.*)

My finished interpretation reads like a news report:

Lenore's Asylum

Part 1: I'm at the residential course, which is, indeed, a social gathering and celebration where I'm happy, and having fun being with friends of like-mind. It's late in the day for me, in terms of my age, to be launching a new career. I am feeling impatient and regret my late start in life. The two teacher Parts of me are familiar but not recognized (dreams and regression hypnotherapy.) The course is a very positive experience.

Part 2: Now, it's time to leave the residential course. I take charge and take responsibility for the Part of me that is feeling needy, lonely, and insecure. This time in my life does not seem to be especially friendly, loving, or comfortable for me. I have feelings of bitterness and regret. Despite how I feel, there is nothing preventing me from moving forward. The path before me is clear. There are no obstacles to me moving ahead. I discover that the needy, lonely, insecure Part of me lives in a place of teaching/learning and healing that has clearly defined structures and rules. The structure of teaching/learning once served the purpose of sanctuary, but the place/time of learning has been abandoned/moved on from. It now feels empty and meaningless. A loss of power has occurred. I am willing to take care of the needy, lonely, insecure Part of me. This needy Part of me, however, does not want to leave the place of teaching/learning that was originally about finding sanctuary from the world. (Association: *I used to own a spiritual/metaphysical/self-help bookstore called Spiritwood Books. The bookstore was a like a cocoon for me at a time when I needed to feel supported in moving along a spiritual path of learning. It was a safe place for me to learn and grow in the company of like-minded others.*)

Part 3: I have an insight. The place in which the needy, lonely, insecure Part of me resides actually feels safe and comfortable. It appears to serve the purpose of growth and transformation (just like the bookstore). The Part of me that brings light to darkness (spiritual purpose) is warm and friendly and provides comfort in this place.

What did you discover?

The dream should tell you something you didn't know. In the case of my dream, it showed me that my experience during the training had triggered me into questioning my path/direction in life! It reassured me by reminding me that I wasn't alone, that my purpose in life had not been lost and continues to be a source of comfort. As you work with your own dreams, you'll discover that it's like learning a foreign language. At first, it can seem a bit kludgy, but over time, you'll start to recognize patterns and themes. You'll discover what your vocabulary of words and associations are, and things will gradually begin to make more sense. You're learning the language of the subconscious mind. That's your internal vocabulary. As you continue to work with your dreams, you'll naturally become more fluent. If you're a hypnosis practitioner, this ability will give you a superpower in your sessions with clients!

You'll find that you have characters and objects that occur in your dreams frequently. It might be your mom, a place from childhood, or friends from high school. It could be a pet or what my friend, Diane, used to call "Greasy Man" -- a shadow character who often showed up in her dreams. (He was definitely worth getting to know!) I frequently dream about cars I have owned in the past. Each car refers to a specific time in my life and reflects my values at that time. In my twenties, I owned a 1967 Mustang. It represents power! When I drive that car in my dreams, I'm in charge of my life and feel empowered! When I owned the bookstore, I owned a Laser. It was my first new car and represents freedom and success. When my old PT Cruiser shows up, it's about my role as a teacher and healing practitioner.

You may find that you have regulars in your cast of characters and movie sets. It could be your spouse, a parent, a child, an ex, or Matt Damon! Whoever it is, realize they're showing up in *your* dream for a reason. As you work with these symbols, you'll discover things about yourself you never knew! Each character or object in your dream will have certain qualities associated with it. They might have a function. A function is like a job -- it has something to do with "doing" something. Exploring is a function. Healing is a function. Teaching is a function. Even avoiding is a function -- a *protective* function! This gives you an idea of what purpose that Part might be serving. A dream character or object might have more to do with feelings.

The most important feeling in a dream is emotion. Emotions are feelings like anger, sadness, and joy. Emotions are pure subconscious communication that can be expressed as colors. We feel our feelings in our body as either comfortable or uncomfortable sensations. What does the color red feel like? What does it feel like to be blue? There's a reason we say, "green with envy"!

Summary

Dreams reflect what's going on in your life at a subconscious level of mind. They can reveal unresolved conflicts, fear, and inadequacies by showing us Parts of ourselves that we may not be aware of.

When all our Parts are working together harmoniously, as an integrated whole, we feel good. When we feel good, we tend to act in ways that support health, wealth, and happiness. When Parts of us are in conflict and fighting for control, we're out of alignment. There's a battle going on inside that can cause problems in our waking life. These conflicts find their way into our dream life.

Your dreams can point out where you're blocked and why you're getting stuck. They can even show you how to get unstuck. Your dreams will also show you the Parts of you that express as positive qualities that you may not be acknowledging. They can also show you where your path of fulfillment lies by pointing out gifts, abilities, and talents you may not even be aware of. Your dreams can point you in the direction of your life purpose and greater fulfillment.

The Dream Walk is a way of getting an overview of the story. It gives you an idea or what the dream is about. It also helps you to identify the Parts of you are involved in the story. This is the first step in creating change is taking ownership of your Parts.

The Dream Walk follows these three steps:

1) Identify the character, object, and action words.
2) Find three words to describe the Part as either a quality, function, or feeling. What's another way of saying that?
3) Walk through your dream by reading it or writing it out using the phrase, "The Part of me . . ."

If you get stuck for words, use a thesaurus. Dream dictionaries are useful for looking up archetypal meanings and gaining confirmation *after* you have interpreted your dream.

If you want clear answers, stay with the dream. Following associations can get you stuck in the mud of thinking too much! Stay with how it feels. If a word feels right, that's your word! Don't overthink. When you get that "click" or "yes!" you nailed it!

The dream should tell you something you didn't know. Dreams are meant to be helpful. What did you discover?

The Inquiry Method

Transformation comes from the inside. The Inquiry Method helps you to associate back into the dream so that you can learn directly from dream characters and objects. It is a practice in active listening that sets the stage for transformation to happen organically. All you need to do is listen to what your innermost self has to say. If you pay attention, the subconscious mind will tell you what you most need to know. This is simplest technique to learn -- unless you're a hypnosis practitioner.

Hypnosis practitioners are taught how to deliver suggestions. We're taught how to talk -- not listen. But in a therapy or dream coaching session, listening is your most valuable tool. Your job is to let the subconscious mind tell its story by avoiding the temptation to try to figure anything out or come up with answers. Instead, admit that you don't know and get curious. Let the dream speak because dreams don't show us what we already know. They show us what the conscious mind either didn't have time for or didn't want to deal with. Something happened to cause you to have this dream. What happened?

Consciously, you may not know what triggered you to have the dream because, at the time, you were distracted or feeling stressedout, upset, overwhelmed, or confused. This is why we want to capture all the details. Every detail in a dream is meaningful. Every Part of the dream, whether it's a character or an object, is a Part of you and has something valuable to say. It deserves to be heard. Even a fly on the wall has something to tell you. Is that character familiar or unfamiliar? Is that object large or small? Does it seem obvious or central to the dream, or is it something peripheral? For example, I had a client regress back to an event in childhood. In the scene, he discovered that Dad was having an affair. The boy was shattered! "Dad's cheating on Mom!" he cried. The child was thinking about Mom, worrying about how this might negatively impact her and how much pain it would cause her if she ever found out. As a result, he kept Dad's little secret.

That was the problem. Even though Mom wasn't in the scene from the past, the client's underlying problem had everything to do with Mom. In his mind, Mom was the "fly on the wall." She was a peripheral character to the "dream" in which he was witness to his dad's behavior. Resolving this internal conflict set the client free from the guilt and anger he had been carrying inside.

B = Become

In the ABCs of Dream Healing, B stands for "become." We want to step into becoming the Part and let the Part speak. This begins with the Inquiry Method. Choose a Part you want to work with. Imagine there are two of you present -- the Dream Coach and the Part you have chosen to work with. Then, imagine what it might be like to BE the Part and describe yourself using words that describe a quality, function, or feeling. Write it down. Then, switch. Step into the role of being Dream Coach and ask the Part to tell you about itself. Record what you learn. For example, in Lenore's dream, I worked with Lenore as a central character. I also had a conversation with peripheral objects such as snow, my car, the asylum, the candles, and even the darkness. It's amazing what you can learn when you become the Part. The opportunities for insight and enlightenment are truly unlimited because a dream can have many layers of meaning. You can work on a single dream for several days, then come back to it a month or even years later and discover something you missed.

Getting Started

Pretend that there are two Parts of you present -- the Part of you that's in the dream and the Part of you that's guiding the process. You can then write down your conversation as it happens.

The Inquiry Method begins by inviting the Part to speak by saying, "Tell me about yourself." Then, *become* the Part. Step into the role of the Part you have chosen to work with and describe yourself in terms of quality, function, and feeling.

Here's where the magic is . . . Imagine that your dream coach is an alien. Become the character or object and describe yourself and your situation as if you were talking to an "alien" from another planet. As an alien, you know nothing about life on Earth! This means everything needs to be dumbed down and described in simple terms. Play stupid but stay curious! You have *no idea* what a dog is, what snow is, what a car is, or what night is. What will help you to uncover the subconscious meaning assigned to each symbol is to identify the quality, function, or feeling words that best describe it. For example, let's say you're working with a fire truck - - you begin by asking the Part to tell you about itself.

Alien: "Tell me about yourself."

Fire Truck: "I'm a fire truck." (This tells you nothing!)

Alien: "I'm from another planet. On my planet, we're gelatinous creatures that hang around the drain. I have no idea what "fire truck" means. What's a fire truck? Give me three words to describe what a fire truck is?"

Fire Truck: "Oh, well . . . a fire truck is big and powerful . . . they go fast? (These are all qualities.)

Alien: "Wow! (Play dumb!) Tell me more."

Fire Truck: "Well, fire trucks put out fires, they're there for you in a crisis, they help people, you know?" (These are functions.)

Alien: "Right. How does it feel to be putting out fires, helping people who are in crisis?"

Fire Truck: "Oh, I feel really powerful! Important! Sometimes I feel kind of hurried, stressed-out, you know, but what I do matters. People depend on me." (Now, we're talking!)

Notice how we're building on the Dream Walk? "The Part of me that is . . ." What you're listening for is a quality, a function, or a feeling associated with that Part. Unlike facts and features, this tells you something! "I'm a red truck with ladders" doesn't tell you anything you don't already know. But if you were to describe yourself to an alien, you might say, "I'm helpful, fun, powerful, I put out fires (deal with crises), and feel powerful, alive, important, or stressed."

If the dream character you want to step into was a dog, instead of describing yourself as a four-legged, furry animal that barks, you might say, "I'm small (or large), friendly (or unfriendly), loyal (or untrustworthy), protective (or dangerous), happy (or nervous or angry, playful (or annoying), etc." Qualities, functions, and feelings tell you something about yourself that you may not be consciously aware of.

It's always a temptation to try to figure things out. But that brings in conscious mind thinking activity. When that happens, you lose the connection to the Part of you that has the answers. Stay curious. Stay tuned into how it feels. That's where the answers lie.

The Inquiry Method is two simple phrases.

1. "Tell me about yourself."
2. "Tell me more."

If you get stuck or the dialogue process seems to stall, don't start asking questions. It's too soon for that. Instead, echo back to what the Part just told you as a question or rephrase what the Part just told you. Then, add those three magic words, "Tell me more." For example, "So, you're big and powerful? Tell me more." Or, "A moment ago, you said that you put out fires. Tell me more about that." Then, wait. It might take a moment, but giving the subconscious mind a little pregnant pause can give the Part the time it needs to reveal itself more fully to you.

Summary

The Inquiry Method is a practice in active listening that builds upon the Dream Walk. What you're listening for are words to describe a quality, a function, or a feeling.

The Inquiry Method is two simple phrases. "Tell me about yourself" and "Tell me more."

First, choose a Part you want to learn more about. You can choose a central character or object or something peripheral. Every aspect of the dream is a Part of you and has something valuable to say.

Begin by assuming the role of a dream coach. Like an alien, you're very curious and want to know more because you know nothing about life on Earth. Ask the Part to tell you about itself. Then, play dumb.

Switch to become the Part. Step into the role and describe yourself. Then, switch back and forth between these two Parts of you. Record your conversation in your dream journal.

If you get stuck, don't try to turn it into an interview. Instead, echo back what the Part just told you as a question or rephrase what the Part said. Then add the three magic words, "Tell me more."

Alien Interview

The Alien Interview is a dialoguing process that allows you to uncover more information about a specific Part. What you will discover is that this process generates insights! The Alien Interview begins with the Inquiry Process. Once you have chosen a Part to work with, you take on the roles of both the Part and interviewer. As interviewer, you establish rapport with the Part by saying, "Tell me about yourself." Then "become" the Part and let the Part speak.

Once you have associated the client into the Part, you can facilitate a deeper conversation by "interviewing" the Part. The six "magic" questions[8] will give you a great foundation for facilitating a dialogue with any Part. For example, I have chosen to dialogue with the Private School (PS).

WW: "Tell me about yourself. What are you?"

PS: "I'm a private school. I'm a structure that accommodates a higher caliber of learning; quality education that has high standards and clearly-defined rules. On the outside, I appear old -- I was built in the 1950's. (Aha!) I'm made of stone -- solid, dependable, and strong. I'm designed to endure. On the inside, I'm vast. Right now, I'm being used for teaching a well-defined, private system of learning, but that wasn't always the case. I used to be used for healing. I was a refuge for people

---

[8] *Dream Language: Self-Understanding through Imagery and Color.* Robert J. Hoss, MS

who needed to find peace of mind. I was a safe place for healing." (Aha! The school is *me* in the role of teacher!)

WW: "**What do you like about being** a solid structure that accommodates a high level of learning?"

PS: "I like to be useful." *(*Aha! Sense of purpose!*)*

WW: "**What do you dislike about being** a solid learning structure?"

PS: "I'm outdated. Well, I'm a solid structure but a lot of my systems are outdated and need to be replaced. For example, the heating system (heart, passion!) just quit. That's why it's cold inside." *(*Insight: I'm feeling a loss of passion.*)*

WW: "**What's your purpose or job as** a solid learning structure?"

PS: "To be an institution. That's what I was designed for." *(*Insight: My purpose is to serve by teaching or healing. Aha!*)*

WW: "**What do you most fear?**"

PS: "Being abandoned. Having no life, no purpose." *(*Confirmation of insight.*)*

WW: "**What do you most desire?**"

PS: "To feel alive, to be useful, to be used to capacity!"

Interpretation: This Part of me that is the private school in my dream has to do with my purpose. Originally, my purpose had to do with healing. (Oh! The purpose of the bookstore was "sharing the journey to wholeness." My purpose *now* is teaching. Aha!) Like an institution, I appreciate order, organization, structure, systems, rules, and guidelines. I need to feel that what I am doing is useful or helpful. The *fear of my* *purpose being abandoned* is a common thread in this dream. Boom! From here, I would dialogue with the heating system because I have just learned that there is a problem with it being outdated; it needs to be replaced or overhauled. It could be a Part of me that I have been neglecting. Or it could be a Part that is overworked and tired. (That rings a bell!) Or it could be something that makes me feel warm and fuzzy inside -- something I need . . .

Summary

The Alien Interview begins with the Inquiry Process. Guide the client to associate fully into the Part, establish rapport with the Part by listening, then use the following questions to interview the Part.

Six "Magic" Questions

1. Who or what are you? (Tell me about yourself.)

2. What do you like about being (that)?

3. What do you dislike about being (that)?

4. What's your purpose or job as (that)?

5. What do you most fear?

6. What do you most desire?

*Last night as I was sleeping,
I dreamt—marvelous error!—
that a spring was breaking
out in my heart.
I said: Along which secret aqueduct,
Oh water, are you coming to me,
water of a new life
that I have never drunk?*

*Last night as I was sleeping,
I dreamt—marvelous error!—
that I had a beehive
here inside my heart.
And the golden bees
were making white combs
and sweet honey
from my old failures.*

*Last night as I was sleeping,
I dreamt—marvelous error!—
that a fiery sun was giving
light inside my heart.
It was fiery because I felt
warmth as from a hearth,
and sun because it gave light
and brought tears to my eyes.*

*Last night as I slept,
I dreamt—marvelous error!—
that it was God I had
here inside my heart.*

~Antonio Machado

Dream Coaching

You can conduct a Dream Coaching session with friends, family members, and paying clients using the same Dream Healing methods you use for yourself. It's fun! Whether you're working on your own dream or guiding someone else, the secret to discovering the meaning of a dream is to let the dream speak. Resist the temptation to try to figure anything out. Let it be revealed through the process. If you're a hypnosis practitioner, Dream Healing naturally gives you access to the contents of the subconscious mind, allowing you to facilitate a coaching session for friends and family members who, normally, you wouldn't work with. It's also suitable for clientele who don't want to do hypnosis or dive into events from the past.

The intake for a Dream Coaching session depends on your purpose for facilitating it. If the client's purpose is recreational, for the purpose of exploration and understanding, you can dive right into the dream coaching session. A laser coaching session fits nicely into the standard 55-minute counseling hour. Just follow the eight-step protocol in this chapter.

While Dream Healing doesn't require a therapeutic goal but it doesn't hurt to ask, "What would you like to achieve as a result of exploring your dream?" Dreams naturally bring to light internal conflicts, inner blocks, fears and inadequacies, and unresolved issues from childhood. Dreams show us what the subconscious mind feels is important. If you're a hypnosis practitioner, when a client brings you a dream, feel excited! They're bringing you a gift from their subconscious mind. This is pure, unadulterated subconscious communication that can help you to pinpoint the "real" problem. This information can help and guide you in facilitating the healing process.

Resolve Bad Dreams

There's extensive research to confirm that two out of every three dreams are "bad" dreams. If the client's purpose is therapeutic, for example, to resolve a recurring nightmare, you would follow the same eight-step protocol but to resolve the problem may require additional skills such as hypnotherapy. In this case, take a history of the problem. How long has it been a problem? Identify how the problem is expressing as symptoms. Why is this a problem? Then, establish a therapeutic goal. This gives you a way to measure success.[9]

Barometer for Ongoing Therapy

Client dreams can give you a barometer for ongoing therapy. Consulting your client's dreams can empower you because the subconscious mind will tell you what needs to happen next. For example, dreams give you a way to gauge the client's progress, identify things that might have been missed in a previous session, locate deeper layers calling for healing, and celebrate success! A really juicy dream can give you a back door to locating the underlying cause of the problem.

Create a Dream

If you're a hypnosis practitioner, you can create a dream and invite the client to step into this. You already know how to do this. Every time you suggest to a client to "imagine a scene", or "find yourself in a

---

[9] Learn how to conduct the intake process in ***Ditch the Script***: *Get Everything You Need from the Client for Successful Hypnotherapy and Set Up to Wrap Up with Results*

situation", you're inviting them to "create" a dream. When you invite them to sense, see, feel, and know that they're there, you're inviting them to step into dream.

The trick is creating a dream is to be artfully vague. Don't impose a lot of detail. Provide the framework and let the subconscious mind fill in the details. I've taken courses in guided imagery and frankly, it's a waste of time. You don't need to provide a lot of detail. You need to invite the client to create the scene, situation, or event in their own mind. The client doesn't have to visualize anything -- just sense, feel, or know. If they think that they can't imagine, prove to them that they're mistaken. Ask them to describe their car to you. How do they know that it's their car? When they walk out of the grocery store, how do they find it? Not everyone can visualize, but everyone can imagine. That's what a thought is. It's how we picture something. We can see, sense, hear, feel, and know that it's there.

There's Rules!

Before you dive into working with other people's dreams, you need to establish the rules. The six rules of Dream Healing are more like attitudes that you carry into your dream coaching sessions, or any healing session, for that matter. Share these rules with your coaching client before you go to work on interpreting their dream. This will help to make it safe for your clients to share freely with you. If you're a hypnosis practitioner, this matches your educational pre-talk.

Rule 1. There's no such thing as a bad dream. All dreams are sent in service of health and wholeness. They serve a positive purpose and are meant to help and guide us. Dreams show us the contents of the subconscious mind. The subconscious mind's Prime Directive is to protect. It's not the enemy. It wants what you want -- to feel good.

Whatever it's showing you, it's doing so for a very good reason. All dreams are good -- even the bad ones!

Rule 2. It's your dream! The only person who can tell, with any certainty, what your dream means is *you*. Forget dream dictionaries! They'll only confuse you. When working with a dream partner, the goal is not to interpret the dream for them. It's to guide them to discover what the dream means for them. Dream Healing is a process of self-discovery and self-empowerment.

Rule 3. Own your perceptions. When sharing feedback, preface your comment with the following five words: "If that were my dream . . ."

Rule 4. Dreams can have multiple meanings. Dreams have many Parts and each Part has its own point of view. They can show you different ways of looking at a problem, offer different strategies or potential solutions, and provide insight into the many aspects contributing to a problem. Dreams seldom mean just one thing.

Rule 5. If you think you know what the dream means, think again! Dreams don't tell us what we already know. This is why Dream Healing is a practice of listening. It's about paying attention to what your innermost self has to say, not telling it what to do. If you listen, the subconscious mind will tell you what you most need to know.

Rule #6. What happens in Vegas stays in Vegas! When a person invites you into their dream, they are exposing a vulnerable part of themselves. Make it safe to allow intimacy by establishing an agreement for confidentiality.

Laser Dream Coaching Protocol

Once you have established the rules, invite the client to share their dream from beginning to end. You don't have to do anything with the dream, yet. For now, just listen. You're establishing rapport with the conscious mind. This is what's on the client's mind and they're itching to share it with you. Let them. This matches the process of recording your dream in your dream journal. You're laying the dream out on the table so that, together, you can explore what's inside the dream. In a hypnosis session, this matches the preliminary uncovering process, which includes the intake process.

Step 1: A = All That I See . . .

Invite the client to tell the story. People tend to share their dreams in past tense. That's okay. Later, when you guide them to step into the dream, you will instruct them to retell the story using present-tense language. But you can begin the process of guiding the client to use present tense language if it seems appropriate. Sometimes, all that's required is a few gentle prompts such as, "So, you're driving down the street and you notice your ex . . . What happens next?"

As the client shares their dream with you, they are "uploading" the data you want to work with. If you invite them to use present-tense language now, they will begin the process of stepping into the dream. As you listen, make note of how the story unfolds and any keywords the client uses. What characters or objects are showing up in the dream? Where's all the action? How does the client describe that Part of them? Watch for quality, function, and feeling words. How does it begin? How does it end? Most importantly, what feelings are associated with the dream narrative?

72-Hour Clause

Once the client has shared their dream with you, ask, "What do you think this dream is about?" or "What, if anything, does it remind you of?" Is there anything about the dream that feels familiar? The conscious mind may not have all the answers, but insights can bubble up as the dream is shared. What's been going on in the client's waking life over the past 24 to 72 hours? What might have happened to cause them to have this dream? Was there a triggering event? Is there an issue that the client has been ruminating over? Where have they been focusing their attention, primarily? Often, the client will have insight into what the dream is *about*. They just won't know what it's telling them.

Step 2: Choose a Scene

Some dreams are short, like commercials. Others are full-length epic movies. When you're facilitating a Dream Coaching session, you may not have enough time to process an entire dream. If you're dealing with a really big dream, you need to chunk it down. Choose one specific scene to work on. You can then invite your client to "step into" that specific scene. Working with your own dreams will give you a good sense of where to step into a dream. If you're not sure, you can always ask your client, "What part of the dream are you most curious about?" or "What part of the dream would you like to explore first?"

Step 3: Associate into the Scene

Once you have decided what scene you want to work with, simply invite the client to close their eyes and step into the dream. Then, using present-tense language, have them describe the scene they find themselves in. Where do they find themselves? Are they alone or with someone? Who are they with? What's happening? What feelings are they feeling as that's happening?

The more they describe the opening scene, the more the client will associate into the dream. This will make more of the details available to them.

Hypnotic Induction

If you're a hypnosis practitioner, you don't need a formal induction because Dream Coaching doesn't require hypnosis. Just help your client to associate into the dream and the hypnosis will happen automatically. But . . . if your client is paying for a hypnosis session, use a formal induction to satisfy their need to know they were hypnotized. If you don't, they may feel cheated.

The best induction for Dream Healing is a short relaxation induction. Avoid doing a long, drawn-out progressive relaxation induction. It's unnecessary and will burn up too much of your session time. Once you have relaxed the client into a light state of hypnosis, you can begin the uncovering procedure. As you guide the client to associate into the scene, they will naturally sink down deeper into the hypnotic state. To encourage this, begin with the broader view of the dream narrative and gradually narrow down to the specifics. For example, "As you find yourself in the scene now, tell me . . . does it feel like it's daytime or nighttime? Does it feel like you're inside or outside? Are you alone or with someone? Who are you with?"

Notice how this line of inquiry matches the basic uncovering procedure of regression hypnotherapy? This approach gradually narrows the focus of attention. This will give access to more specific details about the who, what, when, where, and how of the dream by taking the client deeper into the dream. Also, notice how you're teaching your client to stay present to the dream by using present-tense language. As this happens, they will likely share specific details that they didn't mention the first time.

In a Dream Coaching session, your primary job is to help the dreamer to stay present to the dream. You're facilitating a process of self-discovery. There's no need to try to figure anything out. Resist the temptation to help. That's not your job. Your job is to guide the client and let the answers be revealed through the process. Remember, only the dreamer knows for sure what the dream means! Let the dreamer do the work. Your job is to stay curious and play dumb.

Step 4: B = Become

Invite the client to associate into the feeling of a character or object by directing them to imagine what it might be like to BE that Part of them. Once the client "becomes" the Part, guide them to notice how it feels to "be that . . ." The subconscious mind is the feeling mind. The stronger the feeling, the deeper into the subconscious mind the client will go.

The most important question is, "How does it feel?" If they're with someone, how does it feel to be with this person? This can reveal whether or not there's an emotional charge associated with this character.

When a client connects with a feeling, bring attention to what's happening in the body. How do they experience that feeling in the body? How strong is that feeling? Where do they feel that feeling in the body? Parts express through sensations in the body. If you want to deepen the association into that Part, you need to get more specific. For example: If that feeling had a shape, what would it be? Does it have a color? Does it have a vibrational quality to it? A temperature? If it had a size, how big might it be? How strong is that feeling? If that feeling could speak, what would it say? The stronger the feeling, the deeper the association into the Part, and the more information you'll have access to.

If the client gets stuck, bring the focus back to the scene. Something may be bubbling up to the surface. Allow a little pregnant pause for things to surface. Don't push. Give the Part time to reveal itself more fully.

Step 5: The Inquiry Method

Once the client "becomes" the Part, say, "Tell me about yourself." Let them describe themselves to you. Most of the time, the dreamer will describe the character or object visually. For example, "I'm a fire truck." This is where you play the Part of alien by replying, "I'm from another planet. I have no idea what a fire truck is. What on earth is a fire truck?" This teaches the dreamer to choose more descriptive words that tell you something about what that Part of them is. What you're looking for is how that Part is expressing as a quality, function, or feeling. If the client gets stuck for words, don't try to rescue them. Remind them that you're an alien.

When you want to dig deeper, use these three magic words, "Tell me more." Then wait. Whenever you want more detail, "Tell me more." This is how you make the client responsible for the result. Let them do the work. It may take them a moment. Just be patient. If the client isn't sure, you can echo back to them what they just said as a question. "Your job is to help people? How do you do that? Tell me more." Or try rephrasing or summarizing what the dreamer has told you. "So, you're screaming down the street with all your bells and whistles going off? Tell me more."

If you're not sure about something, ask clarifying questions. For example, "Wait. I'm not sure I get this . . . A moment ago, you said that you were screaming down the street, and now you're at the pub?" Clarifying questions can be used to get confirmation or clarity, and they can generate insight.

Step 6: Alien Interview

Once the client has associated fully into the Part, you can continue into the Alien Interview with the six "magic" questions. Avoid making this a question-and-answer process. Take your time and make the client do the work. When you need to dig down for a more comprehensive understanding, use those three magic words, "Tell me more."

Emerging Process

When you're ready, you can have the client emerge from the dream by opening their eyes. Give them a few moments to reorient themselves, then complete the process with the post-session interview. If you induced hypnosis, add a few suggestions during your emerging process to encourage sleep. Remember, a person who is sleep-deprived is also dream-deprived. This means that they're not getting the physical and psychological healing needed to live a healthy, happy life. Many of your clients are also experiencing sleep problems in addition to the issue they're coming to see you about. Helping them to sleep better can make it a lot easier to resolve their presenting issue. It can also give you a better client to work with by improving their cognitive function.

You can help improve your client's sleep simply by adding a few suggestions during the emerging process. For example, "Notice how much better you feel. Feel relaxed? This is going to help you so much. You may even be surprised to discover how much better you're sleeping. This is going to be so helpful for you because (connect to their presenting issue). You're allowed to sleep deeply, each and every night . . . the way a baby sleeps when it feels safe and secure. And when you wake, you wake feeling refreshed, rejuvenated, having enjoyed a good night's rest . . . having plenty of energy throughout the day. It's natural to sleep peacefully and wake feeling rested and rejuvenated. This is what gives you the energy you need to (make those changes.)"

Step 7: C = Connect

Dreams can provide a source of guidance for daily life. Connecting your dream to waking life allows you to utilize the insights gained from interpreting your dreams in a pragmatic way. C stands for Connect. This step is about eliciting insight at the conscious level of awareness. The question is - - Why are you having this dream? Why now? Situations in daily life can act as reminders of unresolved issues. When this happens, it triggers the subconscious mind to pull out that issue and go to work on it. How does the dream connect to the client's waking life? What might the dream be referring to? What circumstance, situation, person, or experience does this remind the client of? Is there a Part of them, past or present, that feels like this? How does this relate to their waking life?

Step 8: C = Commit

This step is about accountability. Dreams are sent to help and guide us in our daily life. Every Part serves a positive purpose. How might the information gained through the process be helpful to the client in their waking life? If the dream suggests taking action, what new action is being called for?

Make a commitment to taking one small step in that direction. Remember, if nothing changes, nothing changes. What decision can you make based on dream? What new action? Would the client be willing to take action to move in a new direction? This doesn't require sweeping changes. Just come up with one small step. When you take action based on the dream, you demonstrate trust in your subconscious mind. This is an act of self-trust. It empowers you!

If the client is willing to take action, work together to create a SMART goal. SMART stands for Specific, Measurable, Achievable, Responsible, and Time-Based.

- **S**pecific: What will you do?
- **M**easurable: How will you know when you've done it?
- **A**chievable: Is it do-able?
- **R**esponsible: Is it the right thing to do?
- **T**ime-based: When will you do it?

Establish a verbal agreement to do that one thing. Then, schedule a follow-up/accountability session. That's it!

Summary

As a Dream Coach, your job is to let the subconscious mind do all the talking. Give it permission to tell its story. Stay curious. Play dumb. The only thing you can know for sure is that you don't know. The dreamer doesn't know, either. But the subconscious mind knows, for sure. Why not ask it?

Step 1: A = All That I See . . . Tell the Story. Invite the dreamer to share the dream using the present tense. It's all happening now. This helps the dreamer begin the process of stepping into the dream. Make note of key elements before beginning to work on the dream.

Once the client has shared their dream, invite them to think back over the last 24 – 72 hour -- What might have happened to trigger them to have this dream? What do they think the dream is about?

Step 2: Choose a Part. Invite the dreamer to select a Part to work with. It could be a character or an object. It could be something central or peripheral in the dream.

Step 3: Associate into the Scene. Invite the dreamer to step into the scene and describe the situation using present-tense language. As they associate into the scene, more details may be made available.

Step 4: B = Become. Invite the client to imagine what it might be like to BE that character or object. Have them step into the role of the Part and notice how it feels. Associate into the feeling.

Step 5: Inquiry Method. Ask the Part to, "Tell me about yourself." Then listen. Teach the client to use quality, function, and feeling words by playing the part of an alien. Let the Part teach you about itself.

Step 6: Alien Interview. Guide the client through the six "magic" questions. Make the client do the work! Dig for a deeper understanding by using the three magic words, "Tell me more."

Step 7: C = Connect. After emerging your client from the dream, to wrap up your session, ask them, "How might this dream be related to your waking life?" Connect the dream narrative to the client's waking life.

Step 8: C = Commit. Taking action based on a dream is an act of self-empowerment. Ask the dreamer, "Based on the dream, what's one action you can take?" Get a commitment to take action in waking life based on the dream.

You may tire of reality but you never tire of dreams. ~ **Lucy Maud Montgomery**

The Aesthetic Experience

How do you know when you have successfully interpreted a dream? You'll feel it. Either it will tell you something you didn't know before, or you'll have the "aesthetic experience." The moment of understanding will come as a felt sense. This is why we want to stay tuned into the body. Something about your interpretation will just "ping" true for you. A felt sense of clarity that says, "Yes, that's right . . ." or "Aha!"

Look for the surprise! When a dream tells you something you didn't know, you've hit the bulls-eye! That's when you'll experience a moment of insight. Either you'll have an insight into a situation, relationship, or problem in daily life, or you'll realize something about how your own attitude has been contributing to the problem. Sometimes, the surprise will be part of the dream narrative. For example, something happens to surprise you while you're in the dream. There can also be moments of surprise during the interpretation process. It might come on suddenly, as an "Aha!" or as a gradual dawning of realization like, "Ohhhhhhhhh . . ." Regardless, if something comes as a surprise, like "Oh!" you have confirmation!

The Felt Sense

The Aesthetic Moment is the moment you feel it! Boom. If the dream is presenting a warning, it could be an "Uh-oh!" And when unresourceful patterns are brought to light, an "Oh Crap!" moment is not uncommon. Insight can come in the form of an uncomfortable feeling in the body, especially if you have brought to light something that you've been avoiding. If you're facing something uncomfortable, it may be a little disturbing to look at. Bringing this to light might come as a "Woah!" or an "Uh-oh . . ." or even an "Oh, shit!" That's a moment of Truth.

You might feel that discomfort as a clenching sensation somewhere in the body. Recognize that as a sign of resistance. The body knows. When you tune into what's going on in the body, you're paying attention to your biological feedback system. Notice how your quality, function, or feeling words and phrases *feel*. If it starts out feeling fuzzy or vague, that's normal. That's your body's sense of the issue *at first*. It's giving you a general, overall feeling. Just let it be there. As you continue with the translation process, continue to stay attuned to how the body feels. It will tell you when something is right or true. When it's true, there will be a subtle shift, a sense of relief. That's the body saying, "Yes, that's right."

Your "felt sense" is different than an emotion. It's more of an overall sense of something. It can be subtle and more difficult to put into words. It also tends to be felt throughout the body. The felt sense is like a whisper. It will feel like a "Yes, that's it . . ." or, "No, that's not quite right . . ." or "Something like that." It might come as an uplifting feeling, like a moment of enlightenment or awakening. It might feel like you've just made a discovery or a realization. It may feel like you just hit pay-dirt. When you have that moment of "Eureka!" you'll know it!

The body is the subconscious mind. It knows what the conscious mind doesn't know. If you're not sure about something, perhaps sitting on the fence about your interpretation, there's a way to ask your subconscious mind. It's called Muscle Response Testing (MRT.) There are many ways to muscle test, but the method I prefer is easy to perform and works with everyone.

Muscle Response Test (MRT)

There are two steps to muscle testing. First, you need to set up by calibrating for a "yes" and "no" response. Then you can conduct the actual test. Place the thumb and pinky finger of your non-dominant hand together to form an "O." (If you're right-handed, use form the "O" with your left hand. If you're left-handed, use your right hand to form the "O.")

Next, form a wedge using the thumb and index finger of your dominant hand, and place them inside the "O." *Gently* try to pry apart the fingers of your non-dominant hand. This doesn't require any force. You're not testing to see if you can open the "O." You're testing the resistance or strength of the "O."

When you use this with a client, remember to be gentle. It's not a test to see if you can pull the fingers apart. It's testing their subconscious resistance to something. When something is "true", it will test strong. When something is not-true or "false," it will test weak.

Step 1: Calibrate

Before you can conduct the test, you need to calibrate for "yes" and "no" responses. To calibrate for a "yes" response, form the "O", then say, "Body, show me YES." Or just say, "Yes, yes, yes, yes, yes . . ." Then, *gently* try to pry the fingers apart.

Remember, the objective isn't to break the "O" formation. It's to get a measurement of strength. How much pressure do you have to exert before the "O" gives a little? Next, test for "No". Say, "Body, show me NO." Or just say firmly, out loud, "No, no, no, no." Then, once again, gently try to pry the fingers apart. Notice how the relative strength between a true and false response, or a "yes" and a "no", can be subtle. A firm "Yes" should maintain a strong "O." It should take some effort to separate the thumb and pinky finger. A clear "No", on the other hand," should make the body go weak. The thumb and pinky won't be able to resist much, and the "O" will be more difficult to maintain.

Pro-Tip:

Dehydration can mess with your polarity. If you find that you test strong on "No" and weak on "Yes", drink some water. Once you're hydrated, repeat the test for "Yes" and "No" responses.

Step 2: Test

Once you have calibrated for a clear "Yes" and "No" response, you're all set up to consult your subconscious mind. To do this, you must formulate your questions as statements. The body can only respond with either a "Yes" or a "No", "True" or "False", strong or weak response. For example, let's say you had a dream that you think might have to do with a specific situation in your life, but you're not sure. You could make the statement, "The dream is about (specific situation)," and then test for a "Yes" or "No" response. If you get a strong "Yes" response, you have just received confirmation from your subconscious mind. You can now continue to interpret the dream through that lens. If you get a "No" response, test out another possibility.

Body Sway Test

An even easier way to test is the Body Sway. You can use your body like a pendulum! In fact, you could use a pendulum if you're skilled in using one. To perform the Body Sway test, you have to be standing up. Get into a standing position with your feet comfortably apart. Unlock your knees so that you're grounded and balanced on your feet. Then, calibrate for "Yes" and "No".

Step 1: Calibrate
To calibrate for YES, say, "Yes, yes, yes, yes . . ." and notice which direction the body sways. For most people, the body will sway slightly forward as if moving toward something. It's a subtle shift that you can feel. It feels like you're being pulled forward or toward. But calibrate first because it could be different for you. For example, you may find that you sway to the left or right.

Once you have a clear sense of your "Yes" response, calibrate for "No." Firmly say out loud, "No, no, no, no" and notice which direction the body sways, this time. Most people will have a sense of swaying slightly backward, as if the body was trying to move away from something. It's a subtle shift that feels like being pulled back. Again, calibrating is about finding out how your body communicates with you. The movement isn't about falling forward and backward. You're working with your felt-sense, which is very slight and subtle. It might be a sense of shift, a pulling sensation, a pushing sensation, or a slight jerking sensation, either toward or away from.

Step 2: Test
Once you have calibrated for "Yes" and "No" responses, you're ready to test by formulating a statement. For example, "My firetruck is the Part of me that is a helper." Notice how your body responds with

either a "Yes" or a "No." Strong or weak? You can use the Body Sway to test other things, too. For example, if you're shopping for supplements, hold the product against your heart, then test the statement, "This product is good for my body." Try holding a packet of sugar against your body and test. Sugar tests weak for *everybody*! This makes a great convincer by demonstrating the wisdom of the body and, therefore, the subconscious mind.

An Oracle

A dream is like an oracle that speaks to *your life*. It's holding up a mirror showing you the contents of your own mind. Dream Healing requires radical honesty because your dreams will always show you the truth. You may not always like what it has to say, but this is the truth, as your subconscious mind has it. Just remember -- your dreams are meant to help and guide you. They bring light to what is calling for healing.

Dreams don't show us what we already know. They show us our blind spot, the stuff we're not consciously aware of. What triggered you to have a specific dream can often be found by thinking back over the past 72-hour period. Remember -- a dream can speak to more than one area of life. It can point to a recurring problem or a life theme.

When you gain insight from a dream, you may find that the next dream will reveal that an internal shift has occurred. Dream working encourages your subconscious and conscious minds to begin working together on the same issue. This alignment of inner and outer increases internal coherence, which will show up in your dreams. Pay attention!

Summary

Dreams bring to light what is calling for healing. Bringing a dream to conscious awareness gets your conscious and subconscious minds working on the same issue. If you're unsure, use Muscle Response testing to ask your subconscious mind.

*You are the maker of the dream ...
Whatever you put into the dream must be what
is in you.* ~ **Fritz Perls**

Notice . . .

A dream is a story you tell yourself about yourself in the privacy of your own mind. Like any story, most dreams can be broken down into three phases – the beginning, the middle, and the ending. Segmenting your dream to identify the beginning, middle, and end can help you to chunk down when you're dealing with an epic movie. This allows you to work on one piece at a time. Dreams often have multiple layers to them. If you're dealing with a life theme, it could be pointing out several different areas of your life at the same time. These dreams can take more time to process, but they can also offer major breakthroughs if you take the time to honor the dream. Remember, your dreams are all about *you*.

The Beginning

How does the dream begin? The beginning of the dream provides a context or setting with respect to the problem your subconscious mind is working on. It's always relevant to your waking life. It may even be a life theme. This is a good place to dig in because it can provide clues as to what the dream is about. If you can identify what issue the dream is speaking to, the rest of the interpretation process will be easy and flow. What, if anything, does this particular setting remind you of? Remember the 72-Hour Clause. Dreams don't come out of nowhere. Something happened to trigger you to have this dream. What's been going on in your life over the past 24 to 72 hours that might have caused you to have this dream?

Lenore's Asylum Dream: Setting
I am at a party. It's nighttime. There are two guys there. (Association: there were two male teachers). I'm not sure who they are, but they feel familiar. I'm having fun, laughing.

72-Hour Clause
I had just got home from a training program where I had spoken harshly to Lenore for attempting to get me to side with her against a mutual friend.

The Middle
The middle of the dream is concerned with plot development. It's where all the action plays out. This will provide more details about the issue. This is where you're going to find the information about the who, what, when, where, and how with respect to the dream topic. For example, it may be telling you more about how the problem was created, who is responsible, or what some of the contributing factors are.

Lenore's Asylum Dream: Middle
Now it's time to leave. I have to drive Lenore home. It's winter and there is deep snow everywhere. The roads are clear, so it's not a problem. We arrive at a private school. It looks like an asylum. We go inside and there is no one there. Feels empty. The power is out. I don't want to leave Lenore here alone, so I offer to take her to my place. Lenore declines.

Pay attention to which characters are central and peripheral in the dream. Central characters may point to aspects that are more obvious to you. Peripheral characters may tell you more about what's going on in the background. Everything in the dream is there for a reason. For example, the age of a dream character could be pointing to a specific time in your life. A five-year-old child in a dream could be pointing to something that happened when you were five years old or something that happened five years ago. Or it could be saying that you're *feeling* like a five-year-old in a specific situation, such as innocent, vulnerable, creative, playful, or something else. Whatever you do, resist the temptation to follow the association. That will only lead you astray. Make a note but stay with the contents of the dream. Let the answers be revealed through the process.

The End

How does the dream end? This will show you where you're at with respect to the issue or what your expectations are with respect to outcomes. If you're working on a problem, the end can indicate whether or not your subconscious mind has come up with a solution. The final part of the dream may offer a possible solution or indicate that the internal conflict has been resolved. If the dream ends on a positive note, your subconscious mind has likely found some resolution. If it ends badly, your subconscious mind is still struggling to find a way out of the problem.

Lenore's Asylum Dream: End
Snapshot of Lenore's room. It feels like a cocoon. It has a candle burning. Feels cozy.

Lenore's Asylum Dream ends on a positive note. But when a dream ends badly or is incomplete, it could indicate that your subconscious mind is stuck or blocked in some way, or it may just need more time to chew on things to come to a resolution. Trust that your subconscious mind is on the job. It's looking for resources to help you to heal. If there's something about that issue that is still "hanging", the dream will tell you what it is.

When a dream ends without resolution or, worse, in disaster, it doesn't mean the dream is prophetic. It's not a premonition of doom, so don't treat it as such. All this does is act as a negative suggestion that will reinforce all the fear and negativity the subconscious mind is trying to bring to resolution. Work *with* the subconscious mind! Dreams point out where we're at with respect to a particular area of our life. It shows us our expectations or attitudes. If they're positive, that's something worth bringing more fully into your waking life. If they're negative, maybe something needs to change.

By working with your dreams, you are consciously participating in the process of self-healing. Bringing these things to conscious awareness allows you more choices. If something needs to change, you need to know about it. This gives you the opportunity to rethink your strategies and re-evaluate your options. You can then consciously decide how willing you are to commit to a different path. If you need more of some positive quality in your life, now you know! How can you allow more of the good stuff into your life?

When a dream ends "happily ever after", ot may be showing you that you have the resources you need. It could be showing you the next step or where you can go to find help. It could be affirming that success is at hand or that healing is happening. This can help to shift your overall internal energy toward a more positive and resourceful state.

Not every dream will present an answer or solution. A dream merely shows you what the subconscious mind is working on. The subconscious mind may not have a solution. It can only work with what you give it! If the subconscious mind doesn't have a solution, it may need more information. In this case, the dream will reveal this to the conscious mind. If you need to take action or dream abpit it a little more, bringing conscious attention to the issue can help you to begin shifting things in the right direction.

Associations

Growing up, we develop a subconscious language based on our personal experiences. These experiences are then associated with other experiences. This is how the subconscious learns. If something is "like" something else, they form a relationship. Some of these associations may be cultural or familial. For example, Christmas or Thanksgiving dinner, running a red light, or going to church. Ask yourself: What about this seems familiar? What does it remind me of? What do I know about this character or object?

Feelings and Emotions

Feelings are central to the dream narrative because the subconscious mind is the feeling mind. It communicates through images and feelings. As you move through the dream, keep asking yourself, "How does this make me feel?" What's going on in your body? Do you feel relaxed or tense? Is there an emotion bubbling up into awareness? Let it speak! The most important thing to pay attention to is the feeling tone of the dream. Emotion is the language of the subconscious mind and strong emotions can indicate unresolved issues from the past.

Exaggeration

Images and emotions that are exaggerated are there to get your attention. This tells you that this is something important. The subconscious mind is trying to get your attention. It's as if the subconscious mind was saying, "Look at this!" It may be something you're not consciously aware of or willing to look at.

Patterns

Watch for patterns over time. For example, searching for something. Dreams reflect what our subconscious mind is working on. If you don't get it the first time, you'll dream about it again, so pay attention to repetitive dreams or themes. When you identify a theme for the dream, change your working title to a headline. Summarize your dream with a catchy phrase. Give it a headline that captures the essence of the dream. Identifying the theme helps clarify the dream's focus.

Headlining your dream also provides a quick reference for finding a particular dream in your journals. For example, Lenore's Asylum Dream became *"Fear of Abandoning My Purpose"*. This says it all. (I closed my office and classroom shortly after having this dream. Dreams are meant to be acted on!)

Contrast or Similarities

Watch for **contrast** or **similarities**. The mind works through association. What do they remind you of? Does the dream suggest some strength? Resource? Challenge? Opportunity? What might the dream be suggesting? Is there a problem? What solution, if any, is suggested?

Metaphors

A metaphor is a figure of speech or another way of saying something. Dreams speak in metaphors. In particular, watch for **plays on words** when you describe the dream image. For example: "Walking on thin ice." What circumstances in your life feel dicey? "Waiting for your ship to come in." For example, waiting to catch a ferry. What rewards are you waiting to receive? "Throwing the baby out." What might you be discarding unnecessarily? "Pain in the neck." What annoying problem is being pointed to?

Surprise!

Watch for the "Aha!" . . . or "Oh!" . . . "Uh-oh . . ." or "Oh, Crap!" When it comes as a surprise, you're on target! Nicely done!

Art of Dream Healing

When a dream is incomplete, ends badly, or you are unable to gain insight through the Dream Healing process, there are two more techniques you can use to "milk" a dream for more information. The Push Process and Story Boarding techniques work together and provide a way to generate solutions. You can use them to find resources and sources of empowerment when you (or your client) get stuck. This allows you to find your own solutions. They also give you a way to test the results following a Dream Coaching session by revealing expectations or hidden aspects that might contribute to the issue being highlighted by the dream.

To use these methods for yourself requires drawing a series of pictures. You can use a pen or pencil, but incorporating color can help to flesh out more information. In dreams, feelings express as colors. If you stock up on pencil crayons, watercolors, and felt pens, you'll give your subconscious mind the opportunity to express more fully. You can sketch things out in your dream journal but consider keeping a separate book for the Art of Dream Healing. You can buy extra-large sketch pads at the dollar store. These give more room for your subconscious mind to come out and express.

Story Boarding

Story Boarding is a Hollywood term for how a movie is constructed. Movies are built scene-by-scene. This process was developed by Walt

Disney Studio in the early 1930s when animations were all hand-drawn. Essentially, it's a series of drawings, like a graphic novel or comic strip, that shows the story scene by scene. Here we're going to use it a little differently because the movie has already been made. That's the dream. Story Boarding gives you a way to take the whole dream movie and chunk it down into individual frames. This allows you to work incrementally by focusing on specific segments of the dream. In a regression session, this is a skill that will serve you very well when it comes to processing a highly emotional memory. In psychology, it's called "titrating."

Every dream plays out through a series of images, just like a movie film. Each of those movie frames is an image frozen in time. Like a memory, it acts as a container for the meaning it holds for the dreamer. This is why you can't interpret someone else's dream. Symbols are developed through personal experience. From the earliest age, we have been building a subconscious vocabulary that is unique to each of us. Symbols are containers for meaning established by past experiences. The language of the subconscious mind is feelings and emotions. The feeling expresses the meaning held by the dream. Good/bad, friendly/unfriendly, safe/threat. What makes anything memorable is how it feels. Take dogs, for example. If you have happy memories associated with dogs, you probably think of the dog as friendly, loyal, and good. But what if you got bitten by a dog as a child? As a result, the dog might symbolize a serious threat. It could even act as a trigger for a panic attack!

A dream, like any story, occurs in stages. As a result, you can draw each phase or frame of the dream. This will give you a tangible, visual representation of a subconscious event to work with and allows you to "milk" a dream for more information and insight.

The Push Process

Long ago, before digital cameras, iphones, and dinosaurs, I worked in a professional photofinishing lab where we processed raw film for professional and amateur photographers. Invariably, someone would come in with a roll of film that was underexposed. Either they'd used the wrong film in a low-light setting, or their camera was on the wrong settings, and in order to pull the images off of the film so that they could be printed, we had to "push process" the film. Push processing is a way to bring more clarity to an image.

When a dream presents a problem and then fails to come up with a solution, ends in disaster, leaves you hanging, or in any way feels incomplete or unfinished, you can Push Process the dream. This gives you a way to gain more clarity into the nature of the problem, work through to resolution, and bring the dream to a felt sense of completion. When people get stuck, it's usually because, consciously, they're relying on the wrong resources. They're locked into old, outdated strategies, worn-out habitual responses to situations in life, and old familiar patterns and themes that keep playing out like a Country Western tune. Their conscious mind can't come up with alternative solutions because the person feels stuck in powerlessness. That's usually an indication that they've been struggling with the problem for a while. The Push Process gives them a way to find their own solutions. This empowers them to move beyond a perceived block.

What it gives you is a great resourcing tool. You can use it to elicit information and solutions directly from the subconscious mind. If you're a hypnosis practitioner, you're going to love this because you won't ever need a script - the client will provide it. Dreams can provide answers to questions and solutions to problems in waking life.

Solutions that come from the subconscious level of mind are acceptable suggestions. When it comes from the client, this isn't just something you are telling them. You're not just reading them a script. You're feeding back the wisdom of their innermost self. That's potent stuff! Plus, suggestions that come from within are more "brain sticky." These are the client's own truths. If it's a negative suggestion, obviously, that needs to change. If it's a positive suggestion, that's gold! Gather these insights and positive suggestions during a session because this is the stuff of powerful direct suggestion. Echo them back to the client at every opportunity. If you deliver them as suggestions before emerging your client, they'll go in like a hot knife through butter.

Getting Started

Step 1: Capture the Image
Select a scene from your dream that you want to learn more about and draw it! This requires no artistic ability whatsoever. Stick figures are fine. This isn't about artistic skill. It's about inviting your subconscious mind to express on paper. Don't overthink it. Whatever comes, comes. If it's not an exact match to how you recall the scene, keep going. Your subconscious mind may be pointing out something that you missed while recalling the dream.

Drawing requires right-brain activation and that brings in the subconscious mind. Your subconscious mind knows what the dream is all about. Trust that all will be revealed through the process. For now, just draw a scene. You can use different colors or just sketch it quickly in pen or pencil. For example, I often draw a map of a scene to represent where the various characters and objects are in relation to each other.

Step 2: ABC it!

Once you have a picture of a scene to work with, spend a few moments looking at your finished drawing. Get an overall sense of "all that you see." There's really no right or wrong way to do this. Just pay attention and notice things like the feeling tone, contrasting elements, similarities, associations, patterns, and themes. This is how the subconscious mind communicates.

A = All that I see . . .

Sense the general feeling of the picture. How do you feel as you look at this picture?

Notice all the Parts of your picture. What characters or objects appear in your scene? What grabs your attention first? What appears to be most central or obvious? What seems to be more peripheral or seemingly insignificant?

Look at the relationships between different Parts. What Parts are touching? What Parts are separated by distance?

What are the colors feeling? What are the lines feeling?

Are you the observer? In control? Passive or active? Victim or aggressor? How does it feel to be that?

If threatened and can't control something, where would you like to put it?

Where in the dream do you feel stuck? How does that make you feel?

Imagine yourself finding a solution . . . If you had some power, what would you like to do? If there was a fair solution, what would it be?

B = Become

Explore the specific aspects presented in your drawing. Pick three that seem to get your attention the most.

What are three characteristics of each symbol? Do you sometimes feel or act like these three characteristics?

Select Parts of the dream to dialogue with. Begin with the Inquiry Method. Then, use the Alien Interview to uncover more specific information. What do the Parts have to say?

What would be the next thing that might happen to make the dream feel worse? What would that feel like? And then?

What would be the next thing that could happen to make the picture feel better? And after that? And then?

What is the gift this dream has for you?

C = Connect

What are you discovering? How does this connect to your waking life? What other connections come to light? The process of guiding a client through the Dream Healing process can stir up feelings and emotions. When the client steps into the role of the Part, they may be surprised by how strong those feelings are. For example, a student in one of my classes drew a scene from her dream in which a gunman was shooting at her. When she drew the picture, the gunman was a Goliath compared to the image she drew of herself. As she looked at the picture, she tuned into her felt sense. This triggered memories from childhood.

This is what her dream was telling her. She was feeling small. When you're only two feet tall, grownups are like giants. In a moment of insight, she made the connection between a recent triggering event and how vulnerable she felt as a child. The scene was about being "shot down." And the tears began to flow. This is where tapping is a very useful tool. You can use it anywhere, anyone can do it, and it doesn't take long to release an uncomfortable emotion to feel better. You don't need to follow any specific formula, either. Just focus on the feeling and tap to release it.

Tap on it!

If you're familiar with Tapping, there's no need to follow the Basic Recipe. No eye-rolls. You don't even need to tap rounds. Simply identify the emotion, give it permission to be there, tap on it, then validate any change toward the better. You can learn more about my approach in **Ready for Regression**: *Hypnosis Practitioner's Guide to Preparing Clients for Effective Regression Hypnotherapy.*

1. Focus on the feeling in the body.
2. Name the emotion behind the feeling in the body.
3. Gently tap, with two fingers, on the Karate Chop Point on the flesh side of your hand.
4. Repeat a Set Up Phrase three times. "Even though I have this (scared) feeling, I deeply and completely accept myself."
5. Tap through the meridian points. Alternately, you can stay on the Karate Chop Point, rub the sore spots on the chest, or rub the Collar Bone Points. Everything works!
6. Do a round of tapping on the reminder phrase, "This (scared) feeling."

7. Pause. Take a breath. Then check inside and notice. What, if anything, has changed?

If you notice a shift toward the better, validate it. Tap on "I feel better. I'm allowed to feel better." This gives the subconscious mind permission to allow more feelings and emotions to come to awareness to be released. All gone? Celebrate! You just got your good feelings back! Well done!

If you still feel bad, quantify what's left. Is it *all* still there, or just some of it?

If it's all still there, you probably need to switch to a deeper technique.

If some has been released, but there's still some discomfort there, how much of it is still there? On a scale of one to ten, where ten is the worst that (scared) feeling has ever been, how strong was it, to begin with? Where is it now? Validate that change. Then, release on what's left. "Even though I released most of it, I still have a little bit of that (scared) feeling."

C = Commit
What's one small action you can take based on the dream?

Pay attention to subsequent dreams because your dreams will tell you when there's been a shift.

Push Processing

When a dream ends badly or is incomplete, you can ask the subconscious mind to come up with a solution or an ending that feels more complete and satisfying. Here's how:

First, draw the *last scene* of the dream. Then, ABC it. Get a felt sense of the whole scene. Identify what Parts are central and peripheral. Notice which Parts are connected and disconnected. Become each Part you want to learn more about and have a conversation with them using the Inquiry Method and Alien Interview. Then ask, "What would need to happen next for this to feel better? What would it take for this to have a better ending?"

Use your imagination to "push" the dream into the next scene. The answer will come as an image and a felt sense of "Yes, that's right." The subconscious mind speaks in images and feelings. It might come as a picture or a memory. It might be a full-blown movie or just a snapshot. It might seem like a thought, but if you have a thought, there's a picture that goes with it. That's what a thought is -- it's how we picture something mentally. Whatever comes, draw it! Catch the dream. This then becomes the next scene in your Story Board. Process *that* scene, just like before.

Push Processing invites the subconscious mind to consider solutions that may not have been considered before. In dreams, we can fly. Like Alice in Wonderland, we can make ourselves very small or very large. We can call on angels or guides. We can ride dragons or hot-air balloons. We can discover hidden treasure. Anything goes. You're taking direction from your subconscious mind. The subconscious mind doesn't have any of the limitations of the conscious, thinking mind. If you can imagine it, it's already within you. It's available to you, but you may not have access to it because of a block. You can change your expectations by opening to new patterns of possibility. This empowers you! You are literally re-programming yourself by giving your subconscious mind permission to find a better way, come up with a more creative solution, or access more resources.

Story Boarding

This is how you re-story a subconscious event. You take one step, see what happens, then ask, "What needs to happen next?" Take another step, process another scene, and see what happens. "What happens next?" It might only take one scene to come up with a solution or a better feeling. It might take several. But this is how you get the subconscious mind working *with* you.

You can literally baby-step your way into a better dream. For example, let's say the central character in your dream is a kitten. The dream ends with poor little Fluffy in a state of distress. You process the final scene and Fluffy reveals that he's feeling lost, scared, and alone because she's been separated from her family. That's not a happy ending! This is a dream you'd want to "push" because there's a Part of you that's feeling just like Fluffy -- lost and alone. This Part doesn't have the resources it needs. That's why it's stuck.

What this dream tells us is that the subconscious mind has been triggered to go to work on this particular problem. Whether it's a new problem or a lifetime theme, the problem is that the conscious mind doesn't know about it or it doesn't know how to resolve it. The subconscious mind could be working on finding a solution, or the dream could be showing you how it expects things to turn out. In this case -- abandoned. This doesn't need to become a self-fulfilling prophecy!

To get beyond the block, we need to "push" it into the next scene. Begin with the final scene of the dream. That's where you're feeling stuck. Draw a picture. Get a felt sense of the image you've drawn. Notice what stands out to you about it. What's central? What's peripheral? Process the scene using the ABCs. Then, ask yourself,

"What needs to happen for this to feel better?" Better yet, ask Fluffy what she needs or wants. You can then work together to come up with a better-feeling scenario. What might that look like? What else might happen? When you find the better feeling, draw the scene that would represent that.

Interesting things can happen when you start drawing. It's not always what you consciously expect. For example, Fluffy might say, "I want my family!" She reveals that finding her family would mean she wouldn't feel lost and alone anymore. That's a solution! You now know what needs to happen, what the outcome needs to look like, to satisfy this subconscious need. The question is, how do you get there? What if Fluffy doesn't know how to get there? What if you're drawing a blank? No problem! When a Part is stuck, it's because there's a lack of power. The solution is simple -- provide some power! Ask, "If I had some power, what might happen?" Notice what comes up. Let the next scene emerge. This gives you the next logical step toward resolution.

Remember, the subconscious mind prefers baby steps. *You* may want a giant leap into a new life, but that may be too much for Fluffy. Any attempt to make a giant leap into resolution wouldn't be believable. Usually, when we're feeling stuck, that's the problem. Trying to solve the entire puzzle at once is too much. You need to focus on finding the next piece that fits and then the next. That's Story Boarding. You can then work incrementally, scene by scene, to test those strategies. That's Push Processing. Process the scene you're in. See what happens. Then find the step into the next scene. When you focus on the next logical step, it moves you in the direction of your desired outcome, which means you're no longer stuck!

What's happening is that your conscious mind and subconscious mind are starting to work together, scene by scene, to achieve a better feeling, a better expectation, a better result or ending. You're inviting greater integration and you're doing it in a non-threatening way. If the step is too big, it's going to generate resistance. What we want to do is identify the next reasonable step. In this way, you can start moving forward, scene by scene, toward a better feeling. This instills a more positive expectation of how things are going to work out.

The subconscious mind is the emotional mind. The rewards of change are always going to be emotional. How does it feel to have achieved that? When you draw that scene, use exaggeration to emphasize the rewards of change. This is an amplification technique. When you exaggerate the image, it amplifies the feeling it holds. Make it colorful! Dive into the feeling of what it's like to have achieved that outcome. In Fluffy's case, a positive outcome might look like a picture of a family reunion. Bring in balloons and banners! Make it a party! Does Fluffy like pinatas? How about music? What else does Fluffy want to experience as a result of having made this change? These are the rewards of *allowing* change.

Do you notice how the story just wasn't finished yet? You're changing that. In the process, you're creating a new story about *you*. This changes you. Re-storying a dream changes your expectations of yourself, others, and life. When you change an expectation, it changes how you feel. Changing how you feel changes your responses to situations in daily life, which changes the results you're going to get.

Summary

Push Processing and Story Boarding work together to re-story a subconscious event. If you want to learn more about a specific scene or Part, draw it! Capture the image. Then, use the ABCs to process it.

If you have a dream that ends badly, start by drawing the final scene of your dream, then "push" it into the next scene. Keep going until you find the resources you need, discover a new strategy, or there's a shift in expectations. If you get stuck, find some power. In a dream, all things are possible. Call in another Part that can help!

Story Boarding is a process of re-storying *your* story. Push Processing incrementally moves through one scene to the next until you get unstuck. You might only have to push into the next scene, or it might take several pushes to find a solution or a better ending. Through the process, you are inviting greater integration between your conscious and subconscious mind.

The future belongs to those who believe in the beauty of their dreams. ~**Eleanor Roosevelt**

"This" Dream

A dream is a story. It's a story you tell yourself, about yourself, in the privacy of your own mind. As such, it doesn't matter whether you're looking at a day dream, a night dream, or "this" dream -- the everyday waking dream you're now experiencing -- it's just a story. This means that Dream Healing methods can be applied to waking reality. Have you ever noticed how advertising uses the power of image and emotion to speak directly to a person's subconscious mind in order to influence a person's buying choices? When you look at an image in an advertisement, you're looking at a visual suggestion. Notice how it makes you feel. What does it remind you of? What meaning are you giving it? Advertisers either exacerbate a problem or bring awareness to an unfulfilled desire. Got pain? Take "Numbitol." Do you want to feel more powerful? Do you want to gain control of your life? Buy the truck that delivers the most power, can carry the biggest payload, and will navigate rough terrain. Do you want to feel important, and have value and worth? Buy the prestige model. Do you want to feel smarter? Buy the economy model or the hybrid. They sell you The Dream.

In the movie, *The Matrix*, Morpheus, the Greek god of dreams, tells the dreamer, Neo, that we are asleep, unconsciously giving away our power to the "machine." The machine is the Matrix, the consensus reality we seldom question because it's everywhere. The Matrix is a dream! It's a story we tell ourselves.

Where does the story come from? Programming. Where does our programming come from? Our environment and the people around us, primarily in childhood. Our family. Society. Religion. The Matrix dictates the "rules." It decides what we can and cannot do, have or be, and what we should or should *not* do, have, or be.

The truth is, Reality tends to comply with our expectations. That's because, as a child, we were taught *how* to see. *How* we see decides *what* we will see. Our environment then feeds it back to us. According to Rosalyn Bruyere, author of *Wheels of Light*, our programs for physical survival get installed before the age of four. By age seven, our relationship programs have been installed. By age twelve to fourteen, the Matrix is fully installed, and we think we understand how life works. The Matrix is programming that *tells* us who we must be to get our needs met. It tells us how to be and not-be. It dictates what's possible -- based on past experiences -- which then decides how we will perceive ourselves, others, and the world around us.

A dream is a story we tell ourselves about how life works. The problem is that most of us have been programmed with erroneous and limiting beliefs. Abraham-Hicks says that the story with the most emotion wins the race for manifestation. These stories have their roots in childhood. Unfortunately, they can become self-fulfilling prophecies. Think about it. People once believed the world was flat. And so, it was. As a result, no one ventured too far from land for fear of sailing off the edge of the world.

"All that I see . . ."

"This" dream is the ultimate experience in lucid dreaming. It serves the same function as any night dream -- to bring to consciousness what you don't want to look at. Think of the world you see as a kind of feedback system. All that you see -- all that you *can* see -- are the contents of your own mind.

Our perceptions create feelings. Feelings creates thoughts. Well-practiced thoughts become beliefs and our beliefs decide what we're going to get in life. The net result is what we call Reality.

- "I'll never amount to anything."
- "I'm worthless."
- "I'm stupid."
- "No matter how hard I try, it's never enough."
- "I'm not enough."
- "I'm un-loveable."
- "All the men/women in my family get cancer."
- "Men are . . ."
- "Women are . . ."
- "Life is . . ."

If you don't like what you see, change your perception of it. All that you're seeing are your thoughts, feelings, beliefs, values, and expectations. All your fears and insecurities, as well as your needs, wants, and desires, are right there in front of you. They're a result of *how* you see. If this seems like too big a pill to swallow, ask yourself -- What if all this was just a dream? What might it be telling me? If it was actually there to help and guide me, what might it be showing me? What might it be teaching me? How might it be helpful? The challenge then becomes one of interpretation.

Pro-Tip: Be alert for any dream image that appears spontaneously. If you spontaneously remember a dream, tune into it! What were you just thinking about? What did someone just say to you? What just happened? What was the trigger?

According to Julia Cameron, author of *The Artists Way*, sometimes circumstances appear as an affirmation, bringing confirmation or evidence of "**G**ood **O**rderly **D**irection." Sometimes they appear as a nudge calling us to make a course correction. Sometimes they're merely a whisper. When we fail to listen, they don't go away. They just get more insistent. Ignore them long enough and you'll soon have to deal with the shouts! If you've been living a nightmare, realize your soul has been crying out to you. Time to listen!

Getting Started

Think of some small, ordinary activity that you've already done today. For example, brushing your teeth, buckling your seat belt, answering the telephone, walking the dog . . . Imagine that this recent experience is a scene from a dream. What might it reveal about you? What mystery does it contain?

Think back to your earliest memory. It doesn't matter what the memory is or how young you might be, just let the image come. You might find one and then discover an earlier one will come. That's fine. When you have that image, take a moment to get a sense of how young you might be in that scene. Are you alone or with someone? Who are you with? Where are you in relation to those people or things?

Notice the colors, shapes, and position of things, whether they're near or far, left or right, up or down. What's happening? What sounds do you become aware of? There might be a taste or a smell held within that image. Whatever comes to mind, just notice. What feelings might you be feeling? Notice any sensations in the body. What emotions might you be aware of?

Now, take a snapshot of that moment. Take out your virtual camera and take a picture of yourself in that scene. Capture the moment. Take that photograph and place it in a photo album. Beneath your photograph, write a caption. Capture the essence of that memory by giving it a headline. What did you discover?

Dreams are illustrations . . . from the book your soul is writing about you. ~ **Marsha Norman**

Regression Hypnotherapy

Working with my own dreams gave me a deeper appreciation for how the subconscious mind actually works, which helped me to get better results in my regression hypnotherapy sessions with clients. If you're a hypnosis practitioner, it can help you, too. But like any skill, it requires practice. It all begins with you. As you develop your skill working with your own dreams, you'll discover how the tools of Dream Healing cross over to the tools and techniques you're already using. Plus, The ABCs of Dream Healing gives you a protocol to follow that has universal application in your healing sessions with clients. The following are some additional tips to help you in your hypnotherapy sessions with clients.

A Valuable Skill
Dreams give direct access to the territory of the subconscious mind. The subconscious mind is a rich reservoir of resources and wisdom that can be applied in daily life. Too many people have lost touch with their innermost life. As a result, they suffer. To be healthy and lead happy, productive, and abundant lives, we need to give *more* attention to what our subconscious mind has to say. This makes dreamwork a valuable skill for anyone, especially if you're a hypnosis practitioner.

Skill Development

Anyone can consult their dreams to get answers to questions, solutions to problems, and guidance in everyday life by applying the simple tools of Dream Healing. If you're a hypnosis practitioner, Dream Healing can help you to develop valuable skills that can support you in your healing sessions with clients. Observation skills, uncovering skills, and skill working with Parts will empower you in your hypnotherapy sessions. If you're a regression hypnotherapist, Dream Healing crosses over to regression techniques such as regression to past events, the uncovering procedure, inner child work, dialogue work, emotional-release work, resourcing techniques, and insight-generating.

It's All Dream

Dream Healing allows you to view a person's history as a dream. The subconscious mind makes no distinction between real and imagined. As a result, there's no difference between a day dream, a night dream, or "this" dream. All are experienced as valid realities. You can explore a night dream, create a day dream, or guide a person into the past or the future. You can help them make new choices that can alter the entire course of their life simply by changing the lens through which they see.

A Unique Service

If you've been in practice for a while, you may be looking for ways to expand your client-base. You might like to be able to offer shorter sessions, that are more affordable, or avoid burn-out. Dream Coaching is a unique service that you can add to your menu that doesn't require hypnosis. Just decide on a piece to work on and follow the Dream Coaching Guidelines to gain insight.

A Stand-Alone Protocol

The ABCs of Dream Healing give you a stand-alone process that gives you total time control.

1. A = All that I see . . .
2. B = Become
3. C = Connect
4. C = Commit

A = All That I See . . .

A is about finding the underlying perceptions responsible for causing the client distress. Regression hypnotherapy is specifically for working with emotional issues. Rather than merely managing symptoms, the goal of regression hypnotherapy is to restore the client to a state of internal harmony and well-being. This is achieved by addressing the underlying perceptions responsible for generating unhappy emotions and beliefs. Suggestion alone may be sufficient for enhancing performance or temporarily boosting self-esteem. But try convincing a person to let go of a deeply rooted, emotionally-charged problem, and you'll soon discover you're wrestling an alligator. That alligator is the client's own imagination.

Nightmare

To heal a nightmare, whether in a night dream, day dream, or "this dream", the client must be prepared to face it and feel it. It takes consciousness to heal consciousness. The problem is that it can get uncomfortable. As a result, there's going to be resistance to "going there." What the client doesn't realize is that avoidance is 90 percent of their problem. It's *why* the conscious mind can't fix the problem. It's also why the client needs *you*.

Consciously, they don't want to look at those things. But most of the resistance is unnecessary. Some resistance is rooted in misperceptions, some is based on false information, and some is a result of "bad" experiences in the past.

Did you know that you can get rid of much of the resistance in the first session? The subconscious mind's Prime Directive is safety. *Your* job is to work *with* the subconscious mind by making it safe for the client to "go there." First, prove that hypnosis is safe. Real regression requires somnambulism. Make sure the client is actually in a state of somnambulism by conducting a test. Then, satisfy the client's need to know that they have been hypnotized by providing proof that hypnosis is actually happening.[10]

Second, prove to the client that regression is safe. Regression is no big deal. We do it all the time. For example, what happens when someone "pushes your buttons"? You get triggered. You go unconscious and react automatically. When a person gets triggered, their mind associates back into the thoughts, feelings, and learned responses from the past. That's a regression! Associating is how the mind works and how it learns. Why not use it?

The subconscious mind automatically forms connections between experiences that share common characteristics. This is also how the mind remembers. To re-member means to pull out all the associated pieces and re-assembles them. To prove to your client that regression is safe, use a *positive* regression first. Associate the client into a happy memory. There's no resistance to going back to happier times. You can then give the client a pleasant first experience of hypnosis while gathering up some resources you can draw upon later on. Nice, right?

---

[10] Learn how to conduct covert and overt tests in Ready for Regression: Hypnosis Practitioner's Guide to Preparing Clients for Effective Regression Hypnotherapy.

You can learn more in the Ready for Regression First Session System course.

B = Become

B is about paying attention to feelings. The key to deep hypnosis is also the easiest way to elicit a spontaneous regression, by bringing the client's attention to uncomfortable feelings and emotions. The more they focus on the feeling, the more they will associate into the Part of them that is expressing "that feeling." Associating into a feeling is "becoming" the Part so that you can create a newer, better perception.

When you guide the client to associate into or "become" a Part, regression happens automatically because Parts are actual recordings of past experiences. Each Part embodies unique characteristics based on the age at which the Part was formed. The three primary Parts we work with in regression hypnotherapy sessions are the Child Part, the Adult Part, and the Parent (or Offender) Part. When you work with a Part, look for the quality, function, or feeling being expressed by the Part.

Because the subconscious mind makes no distinction between real and imagined, there is no real difference between a day dream, a night dream, or "this" dream. All are valid opportunities for healing. As a result, you can *create* a day dream using nothing more than the client's imagination. You can use a night dream to access memories from the past. And if you're trained in regression therapy, you can use a day dream or a night dream to locate a Bridge to the past in *this* dream.

Once you have established somnambulism, invite the client to step back into the dream. Treat it as you would an actual event and proceed with the basic uncovering process. The moment the client identifies a strong emotion, you have a Bridge. Instruct the client to focus on "that feeling" and count them back into an earlier event. That's all there is to it. You have just converted a dream into a real regression.

C = Connect

C is about evaluating and then connecting changes in perception to daily living. Every client comes to you with a Pain Story. Your job is to transform it into a learning experience and a growth experience – a story of having overcome. To do that, you must guide the client to re-evaluate those experiences from the past, then assign new meaning to them.

Remember the movie, *The Wizard of Oz*? As a young girl, Dorothy Gayle is transported out of her ordinary life in Kansas into the weird and wonderful Land of Oz. She makes the transition from the conscious level of mind (Kansas) to the subconscious level of mind (Oz). The conscious mind is in black and white, very logical and reasonable. The subconscious mind, on the other hand, is in vibrant technicolor, full-spectrum emotion. This is a REM dream through which Dorothy must journey before she can return "home" to her waking life. It's an arduous journey where she meets one obstruction after another (talking trees, nasty witches, and flying monkeys), overcomes her fears (lions and tigers and bears, oh my!), and claims her power. But it doesn't happen all at once. It's not until Dorothy completes her journey and reaches the City of Oz that she realizes she has had the power all along. When Dorothy asks, "Why didn't you tell me this, to begin with?" the Good Witch Glinda answers, "You wouldn't have believed me, my Dear."

"Connecting" is a process of re-storying. The idea is to turn the client's *Pain Story* into an empowerment story. You do that by helping them realize they had the power all along. Insight opens the door to the power of the subconscious mind. You can't just *tell* the client. They wouldn't believe you because what you're saying directly conflicts with their existing story. Trust that the answers are within the mind of the client and let them do all the work! You're there to support, not figure it out for them. Your job is to help them find their own answers and connect what they discover to their waking life. The insights and solutions your clients come up with then form the basis for direct suggestion.

This is the gold of direct suggestion work. During a session, make note of any insights and shift in awareness. Then, before emerging your client, help them to connect what they've discovered through the process with their presenting issue. How will this new level of awareness positively influence them from now on? What's changed? What are the rewards of having made this change? Deliver it all back to the client as "Now you know . . ." statements. These are power suggestions because they're true. This will give the client access to resources that were previously blocked and empower them to accept and allow more change to happen.

C = Commit

C is also about making a conscious commitment to take action. Remember, if nothing changes, nothing changes. Taking action is primarily a test of the client's willingness to make change. If there's resistance to taking action, there's still a block. When insight has occurred, action is called for. Ask the client to consciously decide on a specific action they can take based on what they discovered during the session. The action needs to be congruent with the insights and understandings gained through the session. Ideally, the action should come from the client and should feel easily do-able to the client. If there's the slightest doubt or hesitation, chunk it down. If necessary, reduce it to the ridiculous. The action can even be symbolic. Cleaning out the closet or writing a grievance letter and then burning it can have a profound impact when the action is *inspired*.

The more inspired it is, the more enthusiasm there will be for the client to *take* action, and the more dramatic the results will be. When a client successfully takes action based on a conscious decision, it empowers them. It also acts to reinforce their faith in *you* and your ability to guide them to achieve their desired goal. Their next session can then focus on celebrating success and reinforcing all the benefits of change. This is greasing the wheels of change!

If your client fails to act on their decision, it doesn't mean they have failed. Nor does it mean that you messed up. It's not a report card! It simply means that there's something preventing your client from taking a desired action. That's valuable information! It tells you there's a block at a subconscious level of the mind. You now know what the next step in the client's healing process needs to be! Nice, right?

Total Time Control
You can easily conduct a Dream Coaching session in 55 minutes -- in person, over the telephone, or online. Offering shorter sessions might make you more accessible to more people.

A Gentle Approach
Dream Healing is a very gentle approach to self-healing. As a result, you can relax, sit back, and take more of an observer role in your sessions. It's certainly a way to put fun and variety into your practice!

Help More Clients
Not every client is necessarily going to be willing to dive into regression work right away. There will always be those clients who just don't want to "go there." We all have friends and family members we wish we could help but don't feel comfortable about "therapizing" them. Sometimes, it's not appropriate to go digging into a person's past or emotions, especially when they're a spouse or an offspring.

Deeper Than Suggestion, Alone

Dream Coaching gives you an insight-based therapy you can call upon that is deeper than suggestion alone and that allows the client to find their own answers and solutions.

A Versatile Tool Kit

Dream Healing gives you a versatile set of tools you can use in sessions. You can use them to get the conscious and subconscious mind working together, to uncover internal resources to empower your clients, and as a polishing technique to reinforce healing strategies. You can use a dream to find a Bridge for regression to cause hypnotherapy. Because dreams show us the contents of the subconscious mind, repressed feelings will often make themselves known through a dream. You can uncover these feelings and resolve them just by working with the imagery of the dream, or you can use a dream as an entry point to access a Bridge to the past. You can even use your client's dreams to monitor their progress in a healing program.

Dreams are today's answers to tomorrow's questions. ~ **Edgar Cayce**

That's All Folks!

Dream Healing begins with getting a good night's sleep. While we sleep, the body works on physical repairs and maintenance while the subconscious mind sorts through all the psychological and emotional debris left over from the day. A night dream is pure, unadulterated subconscious communication in the form of a story. That story is all about YOU. It's completely personal and what it shows you is what your subconscious mind feels is important, is working on, and trying to heal. But you won't remember your dreams if you're sleep-deprived. If you're not getting enough sleep, you could be missing out on valuable information that could help you in your daily life!

A dream is a subconscious event. Because the subconscious mind makes no distinction between real and imagined, there's no difference between a night dream, a day dream, or "this" dream. As far as the subconscious mind is concerned, all are valid experiences. Ancient cultures took their dreams very seriously. Ancient Egypt, Greece, and Rome practiced dream incubation to consult dreams for guidance and as a path to healing. Today dreams are viewed more psychologically as a mental process involving memory consolidation and self-healing.

Dreams don't tell us what we already know. They show us our blind spots and bring to light what's calling for healing. Your dreams are all about you and your perceptions. They're meant to help and guide you in your life by pointing out what you consciously didn't have time to deal with, don't know how to fix, or have been trying to avoid in your waking life. Dreams can provide a source of wisdom and guidance by showing you opportunities you might have overlooked or options you hadn't considered. In doing so, they can direct you onto a path of greater fulfillment.

Your dreams reflect what's going on inside *you* -- in your *mind*. As a result, no one can interpret your dreams for you. The only person who is qualified to interpret your dreams is YOU! Dreams reflect what's going on in your life at a subconscious level of mind. They can reveal unresolved conflicts, fear, and inadequacies by showing us Parts of ourselves that we may not be aware of.

Dream Healing is a totally organic approach to consulting your innermost mind to gain insight, find solutions, and resolve internal conflicts that have been blocking you in daily life. Taking ownership for every Part of the dream allows you to transform the dream and, through it, yourself.

You now have everything you need to consult your dreams. You use these same tools and techniques to coach others to discover the hidden meaning of their dreams. It's all in you now!

1. Dream Catching
2. Dream Incubation
3. Dream Journaling
4. The ABCs of Dream Healing
5. The Dream Walk
6. The Inquiry Method
7. The Alien Interview
8. Dream Coaching Rules
9. The Aesthetic Experience
10. Push Process
11. Story Boarding Technique
12. Headlining

Dream Healing isn't merely about interpreting dreams. It's about paying attention to and honoring what your subconscious mind has to say. As you listen, you'll begin to develop awesome intuition while bringing balance and harmony to your mind-body system.

It all begins with you. You now have what you need. Tonight, you're going to sleep . . . Make a commitment now to listen to what your subconscious mind has to say. It will change your life for the better!

Pleasant dreams!

Suggested Reading

Allerton, Scott. *Demystifying Hypnosis*, 2021.

Andrews, Ted. *Animal-Speak : The Spiritual & Magical Powers of Creatures Great & Small*. Woodbury, Minn.: Llewellyn Publications, 2006.

Born, Margot. *Seven Ways to Look at a Dream*. Starrhill Press, 1991.

Bosnak, Robert. *A Little Course in Dreams*. Shambhala Publications, 1998.

Cameron, Julia. *The Artists Way: A Spiritual Path to Higher Creativity*. Uk: Profile Books Ltd, 2021.

Cartwright, Rosalind D. *The Twenty-Four Hour Mind : The Role of Sleep and Dreaming in Our Emotional Lives*. Amsterdam: Elsevier, 2008.

Churchill, Randal. *Become the Dream*. Transforming Press, 1997.

Delaney, Gayle. *Sensual Dreaming*. Fawcett, 1995.

Delaney, Gayle M V. *Breakthrough Dreaming : How to Tap the Power of Your 24-Hour Mind*. New York: Bantam, 1991.

Faraday, Ann. *The Dream Game*. New York: Harper Paperbacks, 1990.

Fred Alan Wolf. *The Dreaming Universe*. Touchstone, 1995.

Gayle. *Living Your Dreams*. HarperCollins Publishers, 1988.

Gendlin, Eugene T. *Let Your Body Interpret Your Dreams*. Wilmette, Ill.: Chiron Publications, 1986.

Goldhammer, John D. *Radical Dreaming*. Citadel Press, 2003.

Hofmann, Albert. *Insight Outlook*. Green Dragon Books, 1989.

Hoss, Robert, and Lynne Hoss. *Dream to Freedom: A Handbook for Integrating Dreamwork and Energy Psychology*. Energy Psychology Press, 2013.

Johnson, Robert A. *Inner Work : Using Dreams and Active Imagination for Personal Growth*. San Francisco: Harpersan Francisco, 1992.

Jung, C G, Joseph L Henderson, Marie-Louise Von Franz, Aniela Jaffé, and Jolande Jacobi. *Man and His Symbols*. Bowdon, Cheshire, England] Stellar Classics, 2013.

Krakow, Barry. *Sound Sleep, Sound Mind*. John Wiley & Sons, 2010.

Larsen, Stephen. *The Mythic Imagination : Personal Quests for Meaning, Healing, and Creativity*. New York, Ny: Bantam Books, 1990.

Linn, Denise. *The Hidden Power of Dreams : The Mysterious World of Dreams Revealed*. Carlsbad, Calif.: Hay House, 2009.

Moss, Robert. *Conscious Dreaming: A Spiritual Path for Everyday Life*. Harmony, 2010.

Moss, Robert. *Dreamgates : An Explorer's Guide to the Worlds of Soul, Imagination, and Life beyond Death*. New York: Three Rivers Press, 1998.

Moss, Robert. *The Secret History of Dreaming*. Novato, Calif.: New World Library ; Enfield, 2010.

Naiman, Rubin R, and Hugh Prather. *Healing Night : The Science and Spirit of Sleeping, Dreaming, and Awakening*. Tucson, Arizona: New Moon Media, 2014.

Strephon Kaplan Williams. *Dreamworking*. Journey Press, 1991.

Sullivan-Walden, Kelly. *I Had the Strangest Dream...: The Dreamer's Dictionary for the 21st Century*. New York, Ny: Warner Books. 2006.

Walker, Matthew P. *Why We Sleep: Unlocking the Power of Sleep and Dreams*. New York, Ny: Scribner, An Imprint of Simon & Schuster, Inc, 2017.

Wendie Webber

With over thirty years of experience as a healing practitioner, Wendie brings a broad range of skills to her unique approach to regression to cause hypnosis.

She is an Omni-Hypnosis graduate, 5-Path practitioner, Transactional hypnotherapist, Alchemical hypnotherapist, Satir Transformational Systemic therapist, and Regression Hypnotherapy Boot Camp participant.

Before hypnosis, Wendie owned a self-help bookstore where she explored spirituality, psychology, and energy-based healing.

Wendie is the recipient of the 2006 5-PATH Leadership Award and the 2019 Gerald F. Kein OMNI Award for Excellence in Hypnotism.

She enjoys an eclectic lifestyle on Vancouver Island, British Columbia, Canada, surrounded by nature, oracles, and cats.

The Devil's Therapy Series

Book 1: The Devil's Therapy: *Hypnosis Practitioner's Essential Guide to Effective Regression Hypnotherapy*

Book 2: Ditch the Pitch: *Simple Proven Client Attraction Strategies for Hypnosis Practitioners Who Don't Love Digital Marketing*

Book 3: Ditch the Script: *Get Everything You Need from the Client for Successful Hypnotherapy and Set Up to Wrap Up with Results*

Book 4: Radical Healing: *Hypnosis Practitioner's Guide to Harnessing the Healing Power of the Educational Pretalk*

Book 5: The Devil's Little Black Book: *Regression Hypnotherapist's Troubleshooting Guide with Tips, Tricks & Even Scripts to Tweak Your Therapeutic Technique*

Book 6: The Dream Healing Practitioner Guidebook: *A Healer's Guide to Uncovering the Secret Messages of Your Dreams*

Book 7: Ready for Regression: *Hypnosis Practitioner's Guide to Preparing Clients for Effective Regression Hypnotherapy*

The Devil's Therapy: *Hypnosis Practitioner's Essential Guide to Effective Regression Hypnotherapy.* Discover how a 200-year-old fairy tale reveals a complete system for facilitating effective regression hypnotherapy. Learn the "Why" behind the "How-To" of regression to cause hypnosis. Turn your hypnosis sessions into healing programs and get results that last. This practical guidebook gives you a step-by-step map you can use to facilitate successful regression therapy. It's much simpler than you might imagine.

> *This is absolutely amazing work. It's so clear and precise, just like a laser. It leaves no doubts about what to do, how to do it, and the best part: Why to do it!!* - **Zoran Pavlovic, Belgrade, Serbia**

The Devil's Therapy provides a simple three-phase, seven-step protocol for facilitating regression to cause therapeutic hypnosis. The first phase is comprised of three steps which effectively set up for a multi-session healing program. The second phase is comprised of two steps which make up the core work of regression to cause and inner child work. The third phase involves the final two steps of testing/integrating all changes followed by the forgiveness work.

Available on Amazon in English, German, and French versions.

Ditch the Pitch! Digital Free Client Attraction Guide for Hypnotists is a beginner's guide to marketing yourself and your services *without* having to do that dreaded sales pitch, figure out how to game the algorithms on social media, or stay on top of SEO. This is an old-school, hands-on approach for healers who want to take care of business by connecting with real people who truly need your help. That's it.

"I've paid a lot of money for business courses and never completed them. I felt overwhelmed and lost in all the content. This course was easy, simple to follow, and taught me so much. I feel confident and ready to change my current system and start implementing what I've learned in my own practice". – **Nicole D**

Ditch the Script: *Get Everything You Need from the Client for Successful Hypnotherapy and Set Up to Wrap Up with Results.* Your success is always going to be in your set up. Ditch the Script reveals simple strategies you can use right away to break free of 'scriptnotism' and start facilitating client-centered regression to cause therapeutic hypnosis. Learn how to qualify your clients, conduct the strategic intake process, and more.

> *I read the first chapter before bed. Wow! Really good! Can't wait to absorb this book!! I didn't think anything could top the first book. After reading one chapter of this second book. I was clearly wrong!* – **Michael Madden, USA**

Radical Healing: *Hypnosis Practitioner's Guide to Harnessing the Healing Power of the Educational Pretalk.* Learn how to prepare your clients for a body-centered approach to healing the mind. Discover how every phase of the healing process involves a contract – from the initial call with a prospective client, to the first session, for the hypnosis, and for regression.

> *Wendie's lessons have been invaluable in helping me to understand the subconscious mind and I feel like I really get it now. I used what I learned right away to great effect with my clients, and it has taken my practice to a whole new level of learning. My clients are seeing results faster! The insights and healing just come more naturally, now – it just seems to flow easily.* – **Craig Homonnay, Australia**

The Devil's Little Black Book: *Regression Hypnotherapist's Troubleshooting Guide with Tips, Tricks & Even Scripts to Tweak Your Therapeutic Technique.* Where *The Devil's Therapy* answers the question, "Why do we do what we do when we do it?" *The Devil's Little Black Book* answers the question, "What if?" What if sh*t happens in a session and you don't know what to do? This companion guide to *The Devil's Therapy* provides proven strategies for dealing with some of the more predictable ways resistance can show up in your sessions with client – and what to do when it does.

> *After almost 40 years of doing hypnosis, I discovered your phenomenal books and online videos very recently and it opened up the floodgates of memories in my career. Your history of hypnotherapy, your trials and tribulations, parallel mine . . . I am going to recommend your books to all those people who've been bugging me to put to paper these principles. I wish I had heard of you years before when I was active, and an industry turned against me because I refused to take shortcuts and jump on the latest bandwagon of change-work for the month.* – **John Petrocelli, USA**

Ready for Regression: *Hypnosis Practitioner's Guide to Preparing Clients for Effective Regression Hypnotherapy.* The Ready for Regression First Session System is based on a five-star rated course. Gain the confidence you need to guide your clients through the multiple healing processes of Regression to cause therapeutic hypnosis.

> *IT WORKS!!!! I just finished a NEW session with a NEW client located in Asia. I had my semi-completed session manual with me that I put together based on your training course and . . . wow. It works. Confidence was back. Client felt great. Deep trance. I could go on forever. In short - thank you, Wendie. I put your course and method to real life and IT WORKS!!!!!! It works!!!! A huge suffocating hug to you!!! Thank you!!! And I didn't even complete all the courses yet!!!*

> *~ Jo Nontakorn*

Get clear. Get confident. Get ready!

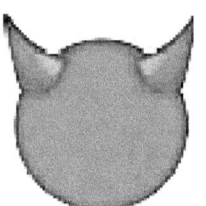

www.ingramcontent.com/pod-product-compliance
Lightning Source LLC
Chambersburg PA
CBHW072015070526
44583CB00015B/1495